OPPORTUNITY ENGINEER

Building the Life You Want with the Tools You Have

by Baylor Barbee

ISBN 978-0-578-62293-4

Design by Baylor Barbee
Edited by Abbey Decker.

OPPORTUNITY ENGINEER

Building the Life You Want
With the Tools You Have

FROM THE AUTHOR OF WINTALITY

BAYLOR BARBEE

Table of Contents

To Dr. Nancy Upton, my friend and favorite professor. Thank you for believing in me enough to tell me the truth. As a result of your lessons and words, I've found opportunities.

INTRODUCTION

Do you remember a time when words were spoken, or an unforgettable event occurred that altered the course of your life? I call them "Ah-ha!" moments. For me, it took place on what seemed like a typical day during my senior year at Baylor University.

I'll admit, during my college years, I was very proud of myself, and not in a humble way. I was a letterman for the football team. I had the same name as the university I attended, and I thought I was perhaps the greatest thing since sliced bread. (Spoiler Alert: Yes, pride does come before a fall.) I was a businessman, I thought. I was the "CEO" of a rap label (that was making no money). I was starting a real estate company—though I had no credit, no money, and knew nothing about real estate. But hey, all the tycoons were doing it, so why shouldn't I? On top of that, I was attempting to create colognes in my apartment by mixing mutual ingredients I found in the different colognes that I liked.

Not only was I doing it all, but I was also vocal about all that I was "going to do". Yeah, I was *that guy*. I'll never forget that day during my entrepreneurship class when, in the middle of me boasting about all the great things I was about to do, my amazing professor, Dr. Upton, paused and, in front of the class, calmly said, "Baylor, if you fail in life, it'll be because you try to do too many things."

My world stopped. *The audacity,* I thought. I couldn't believe someone would tell the Baylor Barbee such things! My ego was bruised—partly because it was said in front of others, but more importantly, deep down, because I knew she was right.

I left class that day with those words echoing through the depths of my pride, determined to prove her wrong. It would take years of trying every business venture under the sun and chasing money, prestige, notoriety, and fame for me to finally understand what Dr. Upton was trying to relay to me with that one sentence.

She—a highly decorated and respected entrepreneur herself—wasn't telling me not to follow my passions or be involved in various ventures; she was trying to help me understand something that I wish to relay to you as well:

Be great at something, not mediocre at many things.

Understanding that concept has had a profound impact on my life and will undoubtedly have an impact on yours as you read the pages of this book. Contrary to popular belief, when I talk about being great at something, I'm not talking about a particular trade, job, or profession. According to the Bureau of Labor Statistics, the average person in America will have between 12-15 different jobs in their life, so putting all your eggs in one basket (or career choice) might not be in your best interest.

What I am suggesting to you is to master something deeper. Learning a skill, trait, or characteristic that is applicable across all areas of your life is the surefire way to progress in life.

But what skill? What should I focus on? What should I master? As I continued to fail at various ventures, those are the questions I asked myself, and you will probably ask yourself these questions, as well. When analyzing the things that worked for me—and more importantly, the magic ingredient shared by all the successful people I knew, interviewed, and researched—I finally decoded the single most important concept that we all must master to reach the pinnacle of our lives:

Opportunity.

We all want it, but not everyone knows how to get it. If we're honest with ourselves, most of us don't even really know what opportunity looks or sounds like. I want to help you change that.

After over a decade of research, application, countless interviews, and observations, I've come to two conclusions about opportunity: First, opportunity is the universal language of growth and success, and thankfully, it's available to us all; second (and more importantly), contrary to popular belief, opportunity isn't a product of luck, chance, or circumstance, but rather is a product of design or procedure. Opportunity is a science. If we can learn to identify, find, create, and execute an opportunity, then we can manifest the lives we dream of both personally and professionally.

OPPORTUNITY ENGINEER

You are the engineer of your life. Your daily actions and habits are the architects of your future. There is power in realizing and accepting this as the truth. Others may do their best to detract from our success or inhibit our growth, but they do not possess the power to derail our futures if we don't allow them to. When a skyscraper is being built, there may be days when it rains, which slows the progress and schedule that the architect and builder try to keep, but do you think that after a couple of bad weather days, the builders give up and say, "Oh, well, I guess it wasn't mean to be"? If that were the case, there'd be thousands of half-built skyscrapers and zero complete buildings.

It sounds silly to think of an architect giving up because of a little weather or other adversity. Why? We know they won't give up because they have a grand goal that has been meticulously planned and designed. They've put in countless hours of resources and energy into the project and therefore won't stop until they see it complete. How much more important is your life than a pile of bricks, glass, and steel?

In this book, you'll learn the opportunity engineering process that you can use in any aspect of your life to maximize opportunities. The process isn't based on new-age philosophy or feel-good acronyms, but rather the same process used by engineers to create the most significant products in the world. The only difference is that the product is you, and the method is based on honing your opportunity finders.

When it's all said and done, don't you want your life's work to be among the greatest in the world? At the very least, don't you want to be the greatest you? You deserve it, and so do the people who depend on you!

The book is broken down into five major components:

1. You'll learn to **ask** yourself the right questions. In doing so, we will look at mental blocks, cognitive bias, and other inaccurate information and glass ceilings that we have led ourselves to believe.

2. We will **shift** our mentality to see new opportunities in ourselves with this newfound knowledge of the limits we previously believed.

3. We will **sharpen** our opportunity skillset so that we aren't going through life waiting on our window of opportunity, but rather we are understanding that we have the tools to *build* our opportunity window. With those tools in hand, we can start to engineer the opportunities we seek.

After those three major sections, there is a fork in the road. Why? While I fundamentally believe opportunity is abundant and plentiful for us all, I'd be a fool to think we can all follow the same path to reach it. Therefore, there is an option to find an opportunity, and there is an option to create an opportunity:

4. In the **find** section, you'll learn how to locate opportunities in places you've missed, how to attack opportunity even when you think it's not there, and how to seize opportunities when the odds are against you.

5. Some of us weren't born with a silver spoon in our mouths. We do not have a vast network, large financial backing, or the best education. Many people live far below their potential because they fall in the trap of thinking that opportunity is only for the rich, connected, and/or powerful. The reality is that the 1% often reached the 1% or have stayed in the 1% because of section #5: the ability to **create** opportunity. In this section, you'll learn how to disrupt the norms, find your advantage in any situation, and ultimately make yourself the DNA of any project, team, or objective you're a part of.

Ask, shift, sharpen, find, and create. You're the architect. It's your life. Opportunity Engineer, are you ready to unlock your potential and build the life you want?

PROLOGUE

After the completion of this book, one of my best friends, Andre Emmett, whom you'll read about in Chapter 6, was shot and killed in front of his home. His untimely death at the young age of 37 is a daily reminder that life is short, and we must take advantage of every breath and opportunity while we're still here.

Rest in peace, Dre.

Andre Emmett
August 27, 1982 – September 23, 2019

ASK

"It's not the answer that enlightens, but the question."
-Eugene Ionesco

CHAPTER 1
LET'S START WITH THE LIES

You're a liar. There. Now, do you feel motivated and ready to conquer the world? I'm guessing that you didn't pick up this book to be scolded and told by a random stranger all the things that are wrong with you, so let me rephrase: You may not lie to me; you may not lie to others; but all of us lie to ourselves.

The next time you're in a supermarket, be sure and walk down the juice aisle and look at the various orange juices and other fruit juices. If you look at them, you'll notice they all have a thick layer of sugar, pulp, or other additives at the bottom of the clear containers and a label that says, "Shake Well before use." The reason for this is that pulp and sugar have a different density than the orange juice itself and over time, start to separate. To maximize the flavor or the orange juice, you must shake it up to get the full effect of the orange juice, pulp, sugar, and other ingredients.

The same thing is true in our lives. In at least some area of our lives, we've been sitting dormant for too long. Our hopes, dreams, ambitions, have started to settle to the bottom because the density of our reality has us feeling like we don't have the glitz, the glamour, the energy, or the opportunity that we once we believed we had. We lost our flavor. The good news is everything you've wanted, and everything you are is still a part of you in the container of your body and mind. You're one good "shake well before use" away from returning to your peak form.

How do we accomplish this? How do we awaken the dormant parts of our personalities and skillsets that we feel we've lost? The answer is in first understanding that we lie to ourselves. Over the next four chapters, we must break ourselves down, ask ourselves some tough questions, shake ourselves up a bit, and then we will start to see it all come together, much like a fresh glass of well-shaken orange juice.

Now let's repeat it, "I'm a liar." Embrace it. It's a positive statement. If you'll buy into the fact that you do lie to yourself, then you'll start to understand that perhaps you're more talented than you realize, stronger than you think, and maybe just maybe, your situation, goal or dream isn't as far-fetched and hopeless, and you might have led yourself to believe.

IT'S A CIRCUS OUT THERE

Growing up in the small West Texas town of Abilene, I was always excited once a year when the circus came to town. My dad always somehow managed to get us backstage, or whatever the equivalent of a being behind the circus tent is. I remember seeing many exotic animals in cages. Lions, Tigers, you name it, they were there. But I also remember the Elephants. The elephants, as giant and majestic as they were, were different. They were different because they weren't in cages. They didn't even have a fence around them, or anyone even remotely seeming to be paying attention to what they were doing. All they had was a small chain around their foot with a stake in the ground. When I say a small chain, I'm talking about a chain and a stake in the ground so small that you or I, in the same conditions as the elephant, could easily pull away and free ourselves.

So, then why can a 13,000-pound majestic animal not free itself? I had to know the answer. I thought maybe they were trained to stay there. I was partially correct but not in the way that you'd expect. You've heard the phrase, "Elephants never forget." Researchers and countless studies have confirmed that this statement is essentially true, as studies have shown elephants to remember people and other elephants that they haven't seen in decades. As amazing as this photographic memory is, it is also the downfall of circus elephants… and of you and me.

When elephants are babies, trainers place that same small chain and the same small stake in the ground on the elephant's foot. For weeks the elephant struggles to try and break free and flee the chains. Realizing it's not strong enough to break free, one day, the elephant quits trying and stores in its memory break this falsity, "If the chain is around my foot, I can't break free." The elephant stores this as an unchangeable truth, and though it grows to become one of the largest animals in existence at over 6 tons, its mindset reinforces its current reality based on old data.

We, as people, do the same thing. If we're honest with ourselves, we all have some area of our lives where we gave up because of how things used to be. We ignore the skills, the growth, the strength, and the experience we have and instead only remember how we used to fail and assume that's just the way it is for us.

In Chaos Theory, researchers study this phenomenon by what's known as the Butterfly Effect. The Butterfly Effect is a theory that states that small changes in the secluded area of a larger system can have substantial effects somewhere else. It was derived from the belief that a butterfly flapping its wings in the United States can set forth a chain reaction of events that ultimately can lead to tornadoes and hurricanes in China.

Yea, I rolled my eyes too. That is until I realized how true it is. Much like the elephants, the thoughts we lock into our minds as limiting truths because of past failures gravely affect our ability to thrive in areas of our life years later. Perhaps you remember the crushing pain of losing the school spelling bee as the judge told you, "I'm sorry, that's incorrect." In your mind, you remember those words and the look on the faces of the crowd as you hung your head in defeat. It seemed like a one-time event, but as a result, to this day, you lie to yourself and say you're not a competitive person and avoid competition. The deep-seated fear of humiliation keeps you from trying again.

Most, if not all, of us have had our heartbroken by a loved one at some point in our lives. Though some recover, many are afraid to open up to others or try again. We lie to ourselves and say, "I'm focused on myself," "I'm happier single," or even worse, we sabotage a relationship when it starts going well because history has taught us, we will ultimately get hurt. We associate love with the hurt we received, and therefore we prevent ourselves from being truly happy in love again.

Maybe you had a pessimistic or narcissistic boss in your first job who found every flaw in what you did and went out of his or her way to criticize or demean the work you poured your heart in to. Though that may have been years ago, to this day, you're afraid to take the lead on a project or put yourself in any position to receive criticism because you subconsciously equate hard work with condescending criticism. Your career potential is suffering as a result. You know you should be further along. But what you don't often realize is that you could be further along, if it weren't for the lies from back then that you took as truth now.

To manifest the lives we want, we must first look at the areas of our lives where we're dormant; the areas where the pulp — our skills — has settled to the bottom. In analyzing the areas where we are stagnant, we must first ask ourselves, "What belief am I taking as absolute truth that might have just been true in one situation a long time ago?"

In asking yourself that question, you're making the first step placing your future and career path back in your own hands by starting to understand that you're wiser now, you're more experienced, and most importantly, you're stronger. The chains that once kept you bound, you're now able to break free of.

The question is, will you?

CHAPTER 2
THE LABEL IS WRONG

At one point or another, we've all looked back at past mistakes and uttered the adage, "Hindsight's 20/20." We are implying that it's often easier to see the truth, or how an event or situation should have been handled, once we're far enough removed from it to view it. Although it sounds good, and it's easy for us to play the "should have, would have, could have" game with our past, the 20/20 view of the past couldn't be more inaccurate.

The simple reasoning behind this is that you're wired that way, literally. Memories are stored in a small part of your brain called the hippocampus. Another part of your brain is responsible for emotion, the amygdala. Your level of excitement, fear, arousal, and every other strong emotion is derived from here. In periods of highly emotional moments, which is often what we think of when we reflect on memories, the amygdala works with the visual cortex of your brain, the part of your brain responsible for sensory impulses from the eyes, to decide what's important. When that amygdala decides something is a highly emotional or "important" event, it tells the visual cortex to remember as many details as possible and to store those details in the hippocampus.

If you look at your brain in terms of a being a camera, the amygdala is the aperture, the round iris of the camera responsible for how much light gets into a picture and the level of depth able to be seen in the camera, and the hippocampus is the film that stores the picture taken. This emotion aperture tells your eyes to focus on certain elements, thus highlighting them, and ignoring the "unimportant" details (which is why we often overlook the red flags).

What am I getting at? Unlike film, in which once a picture is taken, that's how it will forever remain; the hippocampus doesn't store memories as finite, unchangeable pictures. When asked to recall a memory, it recalls the most recent revision of the memory, complete with the most recent emotional data available.

Imagine if every time you looked at a picture of yourself from a vacation ten years ago, the scenery didn't change, but the version of you in the picture changed to be what you are now. That 15 pounds you gained, those extra wrinkles, the new haircut, or muscles you have, all of those are now viewable in the picture of back then. That's what your mind does with memories. It takes the scenario but adds recent developments to recall a composite narrative of what happened, and it changes every time. This means the memory is never finite or final.

Don't believe me? Think about that ex-relationship you had or that former best friend that betrayed you. Before you found out about their betrayal or before that ex turned crazy (it's always them, it's never you right?) You had loving memories of the good times you all shared together and at the time when you looked through photos of you all together you smiled as you reminisced on the great times. Now when you look at those same pictures, do you see that perfect person? No. Don't you ask yourself, "what in the world was I thinking being with that person?" Your perspective changed, not because the picture did, but because your brain received new information that it added to the memory.

This "memory camera" doesn't just apply this to the past; it also does this with what you see and how you feel currently. Hindsight *and* your current reality are never 20/20. They are merely a narrative constructed based on the information you have available.

Since most people aren't aware of these brain functions, they spend their lives letting the brain decide what it thinks is important, and then living their lives accordingly. They aren't in the driver's seat of their own life. If we were to go on vacation, wouldn't you want to decide what you take pictures of based on what you think is meaningful or memorable? Or would you rather randomly click, shoot, and hope for the best?

Understanding that your memories aren't 100% accurate and neither is your current reality can become an empowering asset to you and allow you to see a positive version. Have you ever woken up in your bed and felt refreshed and happy with the world? Have you ever woken up in that same bed, with the same circumstances, but somehow on the "wrong side" of the bed? What changed? Most likely, it wasn't the room; it was your view of it. Perhaps on a stressed day, you woke up thinking about your long to-do list or the meeting with your boss you've been actively avoiding. You also have bills due, and stress creeps into your mind. As a result, when you open your eyes, you're viewing it through a stressed lens, thus saving a memory of a bad day. All that changed was the information you had when your brain took that mental pictures.

We must learn to become expert photographers of our thoughts and minds. We have to quit living lives in the confusion of the dark, and instead, put ourselves in the best possible light.

The late philosopher and legendary speaker Jim Rohn said it best when he said, "Stand guard at the door of your mind."

What you allow into your mind becomes the new setting for the "truths" you recall about past and present situations. If you've ever been to a local fair or stood in front of a house of mirrors, you'll notice the "you" that you see in the mirror is different than how you actually are. If you walk in front of a convex mirror, the mirrors outward facing mirrors you often see in the corners of department and drug stores, you'll notice you look short and fat. If you walk in front of a concave mirror, you'll see the reflection of a tall skinny, coke bottle figured version of you. Which is of these is accurate? Neither. Would you look at either of those and force yourself to believe that you look like that? Of course not, because you know it's not real. Neither reflects how you are. They are reflections of a version of you based on factors that are not you, namely the shape of the mirror.

You must treat your mind the same way. Much like we did in the last chapter, we must ask ourselves, where are some areas where I am viewing myself incorrectly? Tell yourself, "perhaps I'm not as fat, ugly, stupid, slow, (or whatever negative belief you've accepted as truth) as I thought, maybe the mirror is wrong or perhaps I'm choosing to accept an inaccurate version of myself as truth.

One of the leading causes of depression is analytical rumination; the process your brain goes through to solve problems. When we pair that with what we know now about the brain, you'll start to understand that when your mind "can't figure it out," your mind will start adding details, real or imagined, to help you get what you want, "an answer."

How many times have you racked your brain to figure out what went wrong with a business deal, a relationship, or a friendship? Your mind is wired to please you and present to you an acceptable answer so that you can mark your situation as "problem solved". Therefore, when you can't figure it out, your mind adds details or takes composites based on what other people have said about a subject and keeps giving you updated versions of your memory until you finally accept one as valid. Scary, huh?

Think of what will happen if you just let your mind run wild and fill in the gaps as it sees fit and present to you completely inaccurate versions of your past and present to please you or give you closure on a situation? It happens daily. You must not only understand this but start to analyze your thoughts to find those gaps where your mind is using filler information to give you a seemingly complete memory.

PYRRHIC VICTORIES AREN'T WINS

Shortly after the death of Alexander the Great in 323 BC came one of the most powerful warlords of the era. King Pyrrhus of Epirus, a region of modern-day Greece and Albania, began to expand his empire. In 282 BC, War broke out between Rome and cities in Greece. King Pyrrhus saw this as an opportunity to expand his empire and achieve further glory; he and his army set sail for southern Italy to capture Rome. In 280 BC, while heavily outnumbered, Pyrrhus and his men scored a massive victory in the city of Heraclea and boasted another huge triumph a year later in the city of Asculum.

Thirsty for infamy, the King inspired his troops and fought bravely alongside them in the victories. Everyone applauded him as a military genius. However, it came at a cost. The battles had inflicted enormous casualties to his armies. Though he had won the battles, he had lost his generals, officers, great friends, and many soldiers. King Pyrrhus saw the writing on the wall. While being congratulated on the most recent victory, he sadly wrote, "another such victory, and we shall be utterly ruined." He understood what it meant to win the battle and lose the war, and thus the term Pyrrhic victory was born, meaning to succeed at such a high price that any similar victory will cause an irreparable loss.

How many times do we win battles that result in losses? How many times do we fight with loved ones, argue with friends, colleagues, and coworkers, to "be right?" We may prove our point, but our words and actions may ultimately cause a breach of trust and loyalty that we can never get back. Some of us may sacrifice our morals and values "one time" for advancement in our careers, monetary gain, or notoriety. The problem with selling your soul is that you can only sell it once, and you can't buy it back.

The reality is that in each of these situations, the "win" is no victory at all. It's a tragic loss dressed as a win. On the contrary, how many failures, heartbreaks, and other unforgettable "losses" have strengthened you, gave you experience and wisdom, and ultimately helped you progress in life? Those losses weren't losses. They were steppingstones to victory. Often the label is wrong.

We must analyze our win-loss record in life and ask ourselves if those highs and lows are the victories and defeats we once believed they were. Moments that feed our egos are usually defeating. The moments that seemingly break us are victories in waiting.

Whether or not we're a gym buff, most of us understand that lifting weights is an excellent way to increase muscles and help us become stronger. Are you familiar with the process, though? Many of us believe that lifting weights is what directly leads to muscle growth. The reality is the resistance of lifting weights *tears down* your muscles. While your body recovers and repairs itself, the muscles build back stronger, tougher, and more prominent. The loss your body takes leads to the gains that you're seeking.

Along those lines, we often seek growth in our lives: growth in our relationships, bank accounts, happiness, career; you name it. But is it enough to just grow? If we don't correctly name and direct the growth we want, then we will achieve further defeat — even while we believe that we are winning. A bodybuilder may have a goal to gain 10 pounds for a competition, and they might do so by lifting weights. However, if their only goal was to gain 10 pounds, couldn't they also do that by sitting on the couch, drinking beer, eating fatty foods, and not working out? Their weight would still "grow", but is it in the way that they wanted it to?

We must accurately identify what it is we want and label it correctly. A master gardener knows that it's not just about growth; it's about growing the right plants and flowers; it's about focused growth. A gardener knows that weeds "grow," too, but they suck the life out of the plants the gardener wants to thrive in the garden.

Mislabeled victories, negative thoughts disguised as fuel, and ill intentions posed as motivation are the weeds growing in our minds that lead to pyrrhic victories in our lives. Your future can't afford fake wins. We must learn to accurately identify what's helping us grow, helping us truly win, and what's hindering us.

Think about the big wins in your life. Are they moving you forward, if so, at what cost? Are they truly victories? Think about the losses. Have you learned from them? Are they helping you to become stronger? Perhaps they aren't losses at all.

Label the significant events and the current battles of your life and ask yourself this, "Now that I understand I've mislabeled many aspects of my life, what is my real win-loss record?"

If you're honest with yourself, maybe you'll start to pat yourself on the back for those "losses" that you previously had. They're making you a champion.

CHAPTER 3
PROGRAMMED TO FAIL

Do you remember the last time you experienced heartbreak, immense failure, or great loss? Undoubtedly, someone told you to "keep your chin up" – or, even worse, uttered the phrase, "Look on the bright side." In your devastation, you most likely thought, "*That's easy for you to say,*" or "*Easier said than done,*" – assuming you didn't immediately unleash a litany of profanities instead. The reality is that looking on the bright side truly *is* much easier said than done, and science backs this up.

The reasoning behind this, and the reason that we are affected by and hold on to negative memories far more than positive ones is what neuroscientists define as negativity bias. This negativity bias utilized by our brains essentially demonstrates that when all things are equal, negative thoughts, whether they be emotions, beliefs, or tragedies, have a far greater impact on our psychological state than do positive interactions or thoughts.

Whether it's to avoid danger, pain, or failure, our minds are genetically wired to focus on negativity. The whole notion of just choosing to "be positive" is further complicated when you begin to realize positive and negative emotions and thoughts are not equally weighted. What's the ratio of positive needed to outweigh the negative? According to a study by John Cacioppo, Ph. D on marriages that remained stable over time versus those that ended in divorce, the ratio of positive interaction needed to outweigh the negatives is five to one. That's right. You need five times as much positive "energy" to equal or exceed negative energy.

In understanding this, you now have the option to look at optimism as a lost cause since the odds in our mind favor negativity and failure, or you can grasp the importance of the concept we discussed earlier in standing guard at the door of your mind. If you're reading this, I assume that you choose the latter option.

In a later chapter, we will discuss how to jump on the any type of energy and emotions we experience proactively, but for now, let's look at how we can play defense against the negative thoughts that try and creep into our minds and sabotage our happiness and future.

THE "I" IN SELF-DOUBT

There's no I in team is the phrase we've all heard. There is, however, an I in Self-doubt. In fact, "self" doubt is entirely orchestrated by you. We understand that negative thoughts outweigh those that are positive, but how do we defend ourselves against them? The Chinese Military Strategist Sun Tzu, in his book The Art of War, famously stated, "If you know the enemy and know yourself, you need not fear the result of a hundred battles. If you know yourself but not the enemy, for every victory gained you will also suffer a defeat. If you know neither the enemy nor yourself, you will succumb in every battle."

We must treat negative thoughts as an enemy. We must learn to study them, learn their tendencies, and identify how they will attack us so that we can defend ourselves. The beauty of studying these thoughts is that we are also studying ourselves, since it's our minds that create these negative feelings of inferiority and doubt.

So, how is doubt formed? First, we must understand how a thought is formed in the mind. The brain consists of over 80 billion neurons (i.e., brain cells), which are connected by synapses. The brain has over 100 trillion synapses. If the brain were a city, the synapses would be the highways that connect the various buildings (i.e., neurons). With all those synapses firing consistently, it'd be impossible to determine where a thought starts, but what researchers have found out is this: The mind uses its own form of associations to create thoughts, using the context of what it knows to create what it doesn't know. Simply put, the brain uses its own form of algebra to develop thoughts.

Take, for instance, the following phrase. "Last Thursday, the polar bear defeated the Emperor King Penguin in the Artic Arm-Wrestling Championship." Now, of course, it's ridiculous to picture a Polar bear in an arm-wrestling match with a penguin, especially since penguins don't have arms, but you somehow imagined the whole scenario, didn't you? Why is that? You were able to do so because your mind knew the factors involved. It knew what a polar bear, a penguin, and what arm wrestling all were. Using that knowledge, it was able to derive what that whole scenario looked like, even though there is no possible way it would ever see that scenario in real life. If we take it a step further, you probably also pictured it being cold and the entire scene surrounding the arm-wrestling contest, didn't you? Again, your mind takes what it knows, and inserts those details into the scenario to create the thought.

If you look at the last equation, you'll see a simple formula the brain followed: (What we know) X (what we know) X (what we know) = an acceptable thought that our mind creates and accepts as truth. This is because we can account for all the variables. But what happens when we don't know one or more of the variables? What happens if I were to say, "The polar bear defeated the jaskrat in the Artic kinukle championship? You probably drew a blank, right? That's because your mind doesn't know what a jaskrat it (don't worry, it doesn't exist), and you don't know what Kinukle is (again, because it doesn't exist).

How is this relevant to our lives? Every day we face this mental algebraic nightmare that manifests itself in the form of doubt. Self-doubt, at its core, is being caught between outcomes and, therefore, not knowing which direction to choose. Let's say you're unhappy in your current job but receive an opportunity to start a new job with a different company. You lay there at night and your mind starts to run its equation, multiplying together "what we know" which is that you hate your current job, the new job offer's benefits, a stated amount of money, and the required expectation. So far, everything looks good, and you're excited about the opportunity and then your mind thinks about "the other factors," the unknowns.

Suddenly your mind is flooded with new factors to the equation consisting of "I don't know anyone there," "I don't know the culture," "I can't picture myself in the new role." All of the sudden your mind is processing the formula: (what We know) X (what we know) X (?) X (?) X (?) =?????

We know that in math, any number multiplied by zero always equals zero. If we aren't careful, then in the algorithm of our mind, any known thought multiplied by any unknown thought will equal indecision or doubt. Since our minds gravitate towards negativity, if we don't fill in these variables, then our mind will automatically fill in the blanks with the worst possible outcomes. Therefore, so many people stay in jobs they hate, careers they don't like, and toxic relationships that are detrimental to their well-being because they prefer to stick with familiarity. Their mind often creates a catastrophic outcome of any new scenario that then makes the current situation a lot more bearable than the pain of exploring what could be. Before we judge others, we must realize we're all guilty of it to some degree.

How do we combat this? We do so by filling in the variables of the equation, on our terms. All of science and research is based on creating a hypothesis and then testing it, meaning it's all about making an educated guess and then seeing if you are correct. Isn't it far better to fill in the unknowns with positive factors and outcomes than it is negative ones? Let's take the job scenario and fill the variables again. The formula is now (dislike for my job) X (a raise) X (better benefits) X (a chance to meet new people) X (the opportunity to work for a boss who appreciates me) X (the ability to start fresh and immerse myself in a culture conducive to my growth) = Fulfillment, happiness, and career growth.

Will it 100% of the time turn out as expected? Not likely. Just as scientists can't predict the outcome, we can't always accurately predict the future, but I do know this with absolute certainty. Filling in the equation with positive factors and outcomes gives you an infinitely better chance at happiness, growth, and success than does sitting in an indecisive state and feeding your mind with continued doubt.

What factors are you filling your mental equations with? What areas are you stuck in your life and what factors have you allowed your mind to negatively "auto-fill?" Self-doubt and negativity bias will tell you the odds of the equation adding up to the life you want are 1 in a million. At the end of the day, the odds are up to them, but fortunately, the result is up to you.

You become the one who makes it by filling the unknowns in your mind with continued positive energy and outcomes. In doing so, you will see that your thoughts start shifting to those of possibility and begin taking the first steps toward identifying opportunities in your life.

CHAPTER 4
THE GREATEST QUESTION

One of the most famous shows on American television is "Jeopardy", hosted by Alex Trebek. The show features three contestants competing against each other by testing their knowledge in various random categories. The twist on the show is that instead of being asked a question and having to provide the answer, the show provides the answer, and the contestants must ask the right question. When a contestant answers, a panel of judges deems if they are correct. In addition to responding in a question form, they must ask the question correctly by starting their answer with "what is" or "who is".

Life works the same way. The answers are always available; it's asking the correct question that gets us to the levels of success we desire. In searching for opportunity, HOW you ask the question is of equal importance as it is in "Jeopardy", even if the answer is already known.

Let's say you want to start a new habit. (Unfortunately, the "it only takes 21 days to form a habit" myth is incorrect. It was made popular by a plastic surgeon, Maxwell Maltz, in the 1950s who found that after a nose-job, it takes a person, on average, 21 days to get used to their new face.)

The answer to forming a new habit is this: "On average, it takes about 66 days to form a new habit." Now let's look at two possible questions you could ask yourself.

1. How long will it take me to form a new habit finally?
2. How quickly can I develop a habit that will benefit me forever?

Both questions get you the same answer. However, the context of each sets you on two entirely different paths. The first question emphasizes "finally," which suggests to your mind a long, monotonous grind to reach the desired goal. If you frame the 66 days as a long, tedious journey, are you going to be excited to pursue the new habit?

The second option has two critical distinctions. How "quickly," implying it can be done in a short period, and "benefit me forever," indicating that there is long term positive outcome to learning a trait. In that context, trading a mere 66 days for a lifetime of benefit seems like a no-brainer, doesn't it?

Unlike the panel of judges in "Jeopardy" who determine if the question is correct or not, your mind is willing to accept any question you ask it. That can either be an enormous liability that keeps you stagnant in life, or it can be your greatest source of learning and growth. It's up to you to ask the right questions.

If you're reading this book, the answer to the "Jeopardy" of life riddle is: "Maximizing my potential to live my absolute best and most fulfilled life." So, what are the right questions to ask to get to that answer? Even more importantly, what are the BEST questions to ask ourselves?

The greatest questions to ask ourselves are those that break us free of the falsities we once believed and open our minds to what can be possible. Another way of saying it is that the greatest questions are those that help us remove limitations and see the possibilities within ourselves.

IT STARTED WHEN WE WERE KIDS

When we were young, we all played the classic game "Simon Says". If the leader barked out an order prefaced with "Simon says", and you performed the action, then you advanced. If the leader of the game barked a command without saying "Simon says", and you performed the action, then you were out of the game. The game was such a staple of most childhoods that even to this day, if someone yells "Simon says!", then your instinct is to perform the task. But have you ever stopped to ask yourself, "Who is Simon?" or "Why is Simon important?"

As an adult, we fall victim to trying to maintain the status quo or the societal norm. But who sets these norms? What qualifications do they have to determine what the norms should be?

Perhaps we don't know the answers, and while the answer isn't necessarily important, the principle is. The point is that we often accept truths in our childhood and adulthood and blindly go through our lives without questioning how or why we accepted that as truth or gave certain people or situations the seeming power or authority that we've given them.

It gets worse. Because of the programming of our childhoods, we develop cognitive biases that shape how we view the world going forward. Cognitive bias is anytime you create a new reality as a result of your thoughts and past experiences and ignore objective reality. In other words, because of your experience, you see the world through rose-colored glasses. This can be dangerous.

You've probably seen the Disney movie, the Lion King, about a young lion cub, Simba, his romance with Nala, and his growth to battle his evil uncle Scar, who was responsible for Simba's father's death. Along the way, Simba is accompanied by a meerkat and a warthog, Pumba and Timon, as he learns life's lessons during his growth. On the surface, it seems like a cartoon fairytale of justice and triumph of Good vs. Evil. While that may true, that's only the surface. What lies under the surface most likely shaped your view of other ethnicities.

Keep in mind that all the characters in the Lion King are animated animals; they aren't people with traditional identifying skin-tones. Have you noticed, however, that Simba, Nala, Mufasa, and other lead protagonists (good guys) speak in "standard" US English, while the villains in the movie, most notably Scar, have a distinct British accent? The hyenas who follow scar are voiced in African-American and Latino-American accents. The differentiation between good and evil is created with different accents.

Subconsciously, it reinforces the stereotype that Caucasian, or "standard US English" represents good, and accents, whether it be foreign, or minority is a sign of inferiority or evil. This isn't just an isolated incident in the Lion King. A research study by Julia R. Dobrow and Calvin L. Gidney analyzed visual and behavioral representations and dialects of characters in many children's animated television shows. Shows including Flintstones, Scooby-Doo, and several others were analyzed. The results confirmed the bias.

The study found that children's programming reinforced societal, ethnic, and gender-role stereotypes. The heroes were often lean, muscular, and all-powerful. The women were typically viewed as passive, weak, and dependent. In the instances when the women were portrayed as smart (for example, Daphne in the show "Scooby-Doo", figuring out whom the villain was), their intelligence would be undermined by doing something stupid, like hitting the wrong person with a frying pan.

Female villains were often heavier and uglier (picture Ursula from *The Little Mermaid*), while heroines were thinner and more beautiful. Likewise, British, German, and other World War 2 and Cold War-era accents were the most prevalent amongst the villains.

What does this reinforce to children? Standard English, most commonly associated with Caucasian Americans = good. Accents, slang, and dialects = bad.

This isn't an attack on Disney or children's TV, but rather a platform to help you understand that there are often reasons in your subconscious that dictate why you feel the way you feel about certain people or situations. To combat this, we must analyze ourselves and ask ourselves some tough questions. Questions, that if we truly reflect on them, might help us to realize we've been looking at people or situations utterly wrong because of a pre-conceived bias that we didn't know we had. These biases might have arisen from something as simple as a cartoon we loved when we were kids.

Why do you not like the way you look? Is it because deep down you don't love yourself, or has some societal norm made you feel inferior because of a reinforced stereotype of what "good looking" is? Why do you dislike that person in your office? Did they do something to you, or perhaps did they exhibit a characteristic or trait that you've negatively attributed to them because of an experience with someone else? Why don't you think you're smart enough to complete a task, be the boss or start that company? Albert Einstein put it best, "Everybody is a genius, but if you judge a fish by its ability to climb trees, it will live its whole life believing that it is stupid."

The list is endless, and perhaps an entire book could be written on questions you should ask yourself. The purpose of this book, however, is to move you forward, not send you in a spiral of questioning yourself.

So, what questions do we ask ourselves? We must first begin by knowing what area of our lives to ask these questions about. What areas are you currently stagnant in? In which areas of your life do you feel inferior, tell yourself you "can't," or generally feel like you've plateaued? Much like a surgeon using a magnifying glass while performing surgery to amplify the body part that they are fixing, we can place the magnifying glass in the areas of our lives where we struggle. The goal isn't to ask questions for questions' sake, but rather to get to the intended answer. Just like in "Jeopardy", as we discussed earlier, the answer is, "I'm a winner; I have what it takes to overcome any situation or jump over any hurdle, and I'm fully capable of defeating that problem."

What questions do you need to ask yourself to see that as truth? Remember the answer is always there, we must ask the right questions. A common occurrence I hear from people is them telling me, "I've always been overweight," and they usually blame a litany of factors for their inability to lose weight, workout or diet. But let's say the answer is: "I am capable of living an active lifestyle and reaching and maintaining a healthy weight."

What questions would you have to ask yourself to start reinforcing the possibility in your mind?

Perhaps it'd look like this.

1. How has my relationship with food currently prevented me from reaching my ideal weight?

2. What is the true purpose of food and exercise?

3. What small tweaks could I make today that will get me closer to the goal weight I want to reach tomorrow?

4. What are some time-consuming activities (or lack of) that I could replace in my daily schedule with a little bit of walking or exercise?

What you'll notice is that none of the questions were yes/no questions. All of them require a dialogue with yourself. The reason is, shaking off a lifetime of beliefs and biases can't be accomplished without digging deep and analyzing ones' self. You'll also notice the use of subtle words such as "small tweaks" or a "little bit." The rationale behind this to reinforce small changes which your mind views as much more possible than if I were to say "what MAJOR SHIFTS" would I have to make to reach my goal.

When you delve into these questions, you unknowingly start to expose the excuses you previously held as truths for the lies that they are. In Question #1, you might begin to realize that you associate food with comfort. When answering Question #2, you may realize that you aren't using food for its intended purpose, which is to fuel your body. When looking at Question #3 — especially since you asked yourself what tweaks you can make, and not if there are any tweaks — you start to train your mind to find opportunities for improvement. The final question helps you get rid of the most common excuse, which is, "I don't have enough time." Notice that you didn't ask, "Can I make time to work out?" You must be bold and action-oriented when asking yourself questions. This is the only way to keep excuses from creeping back in.

Go ahead, think about an area in your life you are struggling. You know the answer, now what direct, action-oriented questions that prevent you from answering with an excuse can you ask yourself to get you toward the goal you wish to achieve? It's okay to write the questions down. Sometimes it's the only way to see how powerful they are.

You are on a boat in the river of life. Your goal is at the end of the river, and the questions you ask yourself are the current that determines the direction your boat goes. Asking yourself questions that remove biases, pre-conceived limits, and excuses will propel you toward your destination by allowing you to start to shift your thought process into a realm of possibility instead of in-opportunity.

You have what it takes. You are the answer. Now, ask yourself the right questions and begin to move toward the land of opportunity that you've been searching for.

SHIFT

"It's not what you look at that matters, it's what you see."
-Henry David Thoreau

CHAPTER 5
REARRANGE THE PUZZLE PIECES

Throughout the first four chapters, you asked yourself several questions, and now, you may be feeling a bit lost and defeated but strangely free. As we discussed earlier, we had to shake ourselves up to return ourselves to "full flavor".

Now that we've eliminated excuses, realized the lies we've told ourselves, and removed the glass ceiling to open ourselves to the possibility of growth and success, it's time to put ourselves back together again. It's time to replace the former truths we believed with new revelations. These are truths of growth, prosperity, and excellence.

In his book of Psalms, Solomon, a wealthy king of Ancient Israel, said it best, "There is nothing new under the sun." The beauty of life and your current state is the fact that there are no new pieces to the puzzle in your life; everything you need is already there. Too often, we think we need this connection, or that resource, or some other external stimuli to help us accomplish that which we wish to achieve. But the reality is, you already have all the pieces to the puzzle.

Think about the last time you completed a jigsaw puzzle. When you started, it looked impossible. There were pieces everywhere, and you didn't know where to begin. Little by little, you started connecting the pieces, most likely by starting with the frame or some highlighted section of the puzzle. You moved pieces around and tried different combinations until the puzzle began to become more clear. The more pieces you connected, the faster the puzzle started to come together until finally, it was complete.

Now, if you tear that puzzle apart and start over, would the pieces change? Would the puzzle change? What would you have to do to complete the puzzle again? You'd simply rearrange the pieces again to complete the picture. Life works the same way. Anything you've faced, someone else has faced, and most likely, someone had seemingly less than you. Guess what? They found a way to win, and you can too.

The reason we have a "puzzled" look on our face or can't see the finished picture is that we don't take inventory of the puzzle pieces we have in life. What skills do you possess? What resources do you have available? What connections do you have? Have you honestly ever stopped to think about the people around you and what they do for a living, and more importantly, who they might know that could help you?

Just like you can't put a puzzle together without putting all the pieces on the table, Collecting the puzzle pieces of life is the first step. Before we can begin to put the puzzle together and form a clear picture of our dream, we must take that inventory. The pieces are there, I promise you.

Do you remember in the last chapter when we asked ourselves some questions to get to the predefined answer that we had for ourselves? The puzzle piece game works the same way. You can sit here and think about what you want the portrait of your life to look like, or at least your next major goal. Is it a new house, a new car, perhaps a new job, or a spouse? Picture the person, career, or object in vivid detail. Now ask yourself this, what pieces (tools, skills, positioning) would I have to possess to make that picture come to life?

After you take inventory of the pieces that you will need to make that picture a reality, you can perform a "scavenger hunt", so to speak, to find the pieces. Remember, you don't have to create anything; the parts are already there; it's your job to find them and arrange them.

You may be thinking to yourself, "*This is silly; life is a puzzle with ever-changing pieces, and some of the pieces haven't been created yet.*" It's a thought we all have at some point or another; yet it's fundamentally incorrect. You can look at other areas of life to further reinforce in your mind that there is nothing new under the sun. Everything is just a combination of what already exists. There is power in accepting this as truth; your mind can begin to shift toward focusing on the arrangement of your growth, instead of wasting time by trying to create new pieces.

Case in point, suppose I ask you to take out a piece of paper and draw a brand-new species of animal. It must be an animal that doesn't exist, and the world has never seen. Take a few moments and draw that animal, perhaps it's the Jaskrat that fought the Polar bear in Chapter 3.

When you're done, look at your animal. No matter how creative or great of an artist you are, your animal is a collection of pieces that already exist. Perhaps it has legs, wings, hooves, horns, eyes, feathers, fur, a torso, a tail, or any number of body parts, but it's still made of already existing pieces. Though the animal you created is "new," its DNA is not.

Thankfully, opportunity works the same way. The pieces are there. You get to create something "new" with those existing pieces. Too often, we think we must create, which often forces our mind to focus on what we don't already have, instead of concentrating on rearranging, which suggests to our mind that the pieces already exist.

Isn't it far easier to create with what exists than to create from nothing? The same concept is true in baking. There are no new ingredients. Masterpieces are created by combining existing elements. The reason some people flourish more than others is they "arrange their ingredients" better than others, aka, they know how to put the pieces together.

Let's say the famed Cake Boss, Buddy Valastro, and I were to have a cake-baking contest. We were both given the same ingredients: Sugar, Flour, Eggs, butter, and fondant, and both given the same time frame, kitchen, and utensils to bake a cake. On top of that, we were given the same recipe. When it was all said and done, would we create an equal masterpiece? You're probably laughing at the thought of how bad my cake would be. Why was it different? We had the same pieces to the puzzle, the same situation, same blueprint. The difference is that he's done it before, and I haven't. He knew how to mix the ingredients. That comes from experience.

As you continue to grow, there will be times where you're the novice, and sometimes when you're the master chef. At this point, it doesn't matter which you are. What matters is that you start to embrace the fact that the pieces to the puzzle of your life do exist and that you do have the opportunity to find and begin to arrange them to create the life you want.

BUILDING ON THE GO

In a picture-perfect world, we would sit in a Zen-like state and happily collect the puzzle pieces to create a grand picture of our lives. But how often do we live in a perfect world? The reality is that life hits us hard, and usually, we're stressed, overworked, and busy, and we believe that the pieces genuinely don't exist for us. How, then, in times of stress and desperation, do we locate those missing pieces and build the life that we want? How do we find and build upon the pieces when it seems like our whole life is crashing around us?

Over 100 years ago in Billund, a small village in Denmark, Ole Kirk Christiansen sat in his workshop, whittling away at the wood. He loved the art of creating objects from wood. In 1916, he opened his first shop. For the next eight years, his business grew. He made everything from ladders to furniture. However, these were the days before electricity, and one fateful day, his young sons set a pile of wood chips on fire. Ole's shop was destroyed, as was his family home.

Many others would have quit. Ole didn't see it that way. Ole looked at the now decimated plot of land and decided it was a sign that he should build an even larger factory with the newfound space. Though eternally optimistic, Ole faced challenges. The American stock market crashed in 1929, sending the entire free world into a depression. Ole had to lay off most of his staff to keep the business afloat.

Many businesses would close their doors, but Ole saw an opportunity in adapting. Low on materials, he decided to make inexpensive toys out of the wood that he had remaining in hopes they would sell. They didn't. The depression was too strong. His family fought to get him to refocus on making "meaningful goods" and even tried to add a stipulation to stop making toys to receive a bailout loan to bring the business back from its foray into bankruptcy.

But Ole was passionate. He loved working with woods, and he thoroughly enjoyed making small wooden toys. He persisted. Though there was no inkling of progress on the surface, Ole knew toys were what he wanted to make. Despite the resistance, he doubled down on his stance on toy making and renamed his company leg godt, Danish for "Play Well." With his newfound commitment to cheap toys, and his refusal to skimp on quality, Ole's company began to flourish. Around the country, people took notice and started to gravitate toward his wooden toys.

Christiansen's leg godt was thriving, yet disaster struck again. During World War 2, Denmark was invaded by neighboring Germany. During the invasion, Ole's factory was burned down once again. To make matters worse, because of the war, consumer materials such as wood and metal were scarce. Many companies shut down. Ole saw opportunity. Since wood was scarce, he bought the country's first plastic mold injection machine. The machine enabled him to create molds, melt plastic, and ultimately create plastic toys in the shape of the mold. Due to his success with simple wooden toys, Ole knew there was a market for simple toys. He created the Automatic Binding Brick, a simple toy that allowed children to stack and connect the brick in many ways.

The blocks were a success, and though Ole died in 1952, his sons took over and built a full out brick "system of play" that allowed bricks of different sizes to be able to connect to one another in an endless array of designs.

So, what happened to Christiansen's "system of play"? Today, "leg godt", or LEGO, sells 75B LEGOs annually in 140 different countries. LEGO makes over 3,700 different types of LEGOs, which can all connect in various ways due to their simplicity to create virtually any design, including the 42-foot-tall London Bridge replica, which boasts over 5.8M LEGOs and was large enough for real cars to drive underneath.

Aside from the utter resiliency and belief in himself, the key to Ole Christiansen's success was that no matter how bad it got, he always saw the pieces to the puzzle and rearranged the pieces he had to create LEGO. First, he looked at the burned down house and saw a piece to the puzzle...land to build on. When the second disaster struck, he knew he didn't have the raw materials to make large furniture, but the pieces allowed him to make small toys. The pieces were still there. When his factory burned down again, he realized he still had a following, and they still wanted his products (those were the pieces to the puzzle he had), so he rallied on that and made a different type of toy.

Find the pieces, rearrange, build. Find the pieces, rearrange, build. It's a simple concept that Ole and many others throughout history have used to turn calamity into fortune and legacy. The same opportunity is available to you. Look at the pieces that you have and build with those. If your world is crashing down, wait for the smoke to clear, look at the available pieces, and build again.

The pieces are always there. Don't you think it's time to start putting the puzzle together?

CHAPTER 6
THE POWER OF A MISS

A great friend of mine, Andre Emmett, is a professional basketball player who's played in the NBA, overseas, and the Big 3 professional league. Because of our schedules, we typically work out at the same time. Every day, I see him working on his craft, shooting hundreds of shots. Having been the all-time-leading scorer in the BIG XII Conference, winning numerous scoring titles and even scoring 71 points in a professional game, it's safe to say that Dre knows how to put the ball in the basket.

One particular day, however, as I watched him shoot at the gym, I noticed that the shots weren't going in at the rate they usually do. He continued to shoot for hours, and it just didn't seem like it was his day. I figured he'd be frustrated with the lack of makes, but after the workout, he appeared to be in his typical calm collected mood.

I was confused. Andre made his living by shooting the ball, and on a day that wasn't going well, he didn't seem the least bit worried about it. I joked, "Not a lot of makes today," and his reply taught me a valuable lesson.

He said, "It's all good; the misses are just as important as the makes."

I responded, "Uh, Dre, I think the makes are more important."

To this, he replied, "The makes give you momentum, but the misses are where you learn."

Spoken like a true professional. When was the last time you looked at an aspect of your career and applauded the "misses?" Perhaps you're a teacher, and the majority of kids failed the test. Maybe you're a great salesman, and this past month you couldn't close any deals. Most would go into panic mode, but there is always opportunity in the "misses" of life. As that teacher, perhaps you learned to adopt a new teaching style. As a salesman, the slow month revealed areas in your sales technique that you could work on.

The trick is to quit viewing situations that don't go in your favor as misses, failures, or inadequacies and instead shift your attention to the value those situations and circumstances provide you. The misses are feedback. They aren't failure. Consider every miss as merely a part of your own personal sonar system.

Sonar, commonly used by whales and dolphins, uses echoes to pinpoint surroundings. The animal, submarine, or whatever is utilizing sonar emits a sound, and, based on how quickly the echo comes back (i.e., the sound waves bouncing off an object), they can read their surroundings and locate prey. If you've ever stood at the edge of a large canyon and yelled, you know it takes a while to hear your echo because the sound waves take a long time to reach the other side of the canyon and bounce back. If you were to scream in a basketball gym, you'd hear the echo much faster. The closer the object is, the faster the feedback comes. Marine animals are so precise with sonar that they can locate and identify objects as small as a BB from 15 meters away.

Now, what if you changed your mindset to start seeing failure as the feedback in a sonar loop? Every attempt you make – whether it's shooting a basket, going for a sale, or trying a new diet-and-exercise routine – is the sound you put out. What is perceived as "failure" is simply the process of getting feedback faster because it's closer to you, meaning there is something you need to correct. If you adopt this mindset, you'll begin to stop viewing any circumstance as unfavorable because the winning plays give you momentum, and the opportunities that didn't go as planned are only immediate feedback to help you get to your result faster. Focus on becoming highly in tune with your sonar feedback loop so that you will spot the most minute changes that you need to make when you receive "failure" feedback, and, in turn, you can make corrections and flourish.

BEAUTY IN THE VOID

Perhaps you can adapt the philosophy of understanding the importance of the misses and perceived failures in life because we often get another chance to correct it. But how do we handle the areas of our life where we feel we are fundamentally inadequate? What about the areas that go beyond a miss, the areas where we feel like we lack a skill or trait, the aspects of our life that we see a vast emptiness or void in? The answer can be found in one of America's favorite breakfast food, donuts.

Originally thought to have been invented in the Netherlands and Germany, Donuts were then called "fried cakes" or "twisters." Because of the way donuts are fried, they would have a crispy outside. However, the inside would still be raw dough. To combat this, the fried cakes were often filled with fruits or cream to account for this inability to cook the center evenly. However, one day, someone had a Grande idea. What if we cut a hole in the center of the fried cake so that it could cook evenly on all sides, and thus remove the part that was giving bakers trouble? Alas, the modern donut that we know today was created.

The void was necessary for the donut to taste good. The emptiness in the donut was ultimately what made the donut complete. Your life is no different. Too often, we look at what we don't have, whether it be money, resources, friends, relationships, or whatever we lack, and think it makes us less of a person or gives us less of an opportunity to thrive.

What if you found the beauty in that void? What if you looked at what you lack from the perspective of a donut and realized that the void is necessary to make you complete? The money you don't have to start a business can create an insatiable appetite to succeed and an ability to make the most out of very little. The lack of spouse, partner, or relationship gives you ample time to work on being happy alone and to improve on the qualities that will make you a great partner in the future. The lack of a particular skill or trait allows you to be thankful for the skills that you do have and focus on improving those.

Perhaps you aren't the smartest, and it's okay. Consistency often beats brilliance. Maybe you're not the world's greatest athlete. Focus on health and longevity in life. What you'll find if you're honest with yourself is that the perceived void you have is most likely only noticeable to you. Before reading this, did you know that the center of the donut was necessary? We love the shape of donuts. Start looking at the voids in your life as opportunities. Ask yourself, "How can I view this perceived 'lack' as a strength?" When you start to develop a mindset of finding power in what you once saw as weakness, you begin to realize that other people will envy what you have. You have focused on yourself. You "fried evenly on all sides", and, as a result, you now have a mindset and a skillset that can become valuable to the marketplace, your family, your community, or your company. You can fill the void that others see in themselves. In other words, you're the donut hole to complete their donut!

Maybe you're one of the five people on Earth who isn't a fan of donuts. There are several other instances in life that illustrate the importance of the void. Think about boats. They are designed to stay on top of the water. As long as there is air and space inside the boat – and *not* water – then it will float. Boats don't sink because the water gets high; they only sink because they lose their void and become filled with water.

Your lungs, necessary for breathing and life, are most efficient when they are empty. When a person's lungs fill up with fluid, known as pulmonary edema, it decreases the capacity of the lungs to produce oxygen because of the lack of "void," which can lead to extreme health risks or worse. Life is filled with examples of specimens and objects that get their strength or function from what others see as a void.

How do we reshape our mindset to see the opportunity where we once saw emptiness?

Take the burden of perfection away.

Too often, we associate perfection with completion. In a never-ending race to be the best version of ourselves, which is a good thing, we make the mistake of believing that perfection means having it all. That couldn't be further from the truth.

Whether you view it as a religion or a philosophy, nearly ten percent of the world's population practices Buddhism. Buddhism is primarily shaped by what is known as the "4 Noble Truths," which aim to help one alleviate suffering in his or her life. Now, this is by no means an attempt to convert anyone to Buddhism. Nor am I suggesting the entire culture of Buddhism can be summed up in one illustration. However, the premise behind the 4 Noble Truths can be applied to anyone looking to fill the void, separate themselves from the desire to be perfect, and to find strength in who they are.

The First of the Noble Truths states that all of life is suffering. "Suffering" is a loose translation of the Sanskrit word Dukkha, which can also mean "incapable of satisfying." The truth essentially says that unhappiness comes from chasing temporary things. The Second of the Truths is where we start to see the tie-in to our lives in eliminating the shame of the void we feel. This Truth states that the cause of suffering comes from a thirst for greed or desire. Essentially, the attachment we place on things, situations, or ideals are the cause of our unhappiness.

Remember earlier in the chapter when we asked ourselves about how we handle the voids in our life? Perhaps the better question to ask ourselves to break free of a void-mindset is this, "Why do I feel that this is a void, and even if it is, why is the void a bad thing?" We must change our mindset from believing we always need to fill the void. In trying to fill the void, we often turn to external sources. The Third Truth shows us that the cure for suffering is to lose the attachment to those things. Quit chasing external conditions, situations, people, or things to fill yourself up.

What would happen if you had a cup with a large hole in the bottom of it? Would pouring more water in it fix the problem? Would blasting it with a firehose cause it to fill up? Maybe for a second, but what would happen eventually? The water would leak out. How do you fix the problem? You fix the leak.

In our lives, we fix the leaks by understanding that we don't have to be perfect and that perfection doesn't mean completion. The leak is an unattainable desire to fill the areas of our lives in which we find ourselves empty. We must start to view that emptiness as strength. It has to be there for us to function at our capacity. It's counterintuitive, but it will make all the difference in your view of yourself.

EMBRACE THE VOID

Do me a favor. Take out a pen and a piece of paper, and for a second, I want you to pretend that Marvel Comics called you and wanted you to create a new Superhero. Here's the catch. The superpower of that new hero is the very thing that you previously thought was a void in your life. As we mentioned earlier, perhaps you view a lack of money as your void? Wouldn't your superhero be the ultimate hard worker to help him/herself and others free themselves from the financial burden? What might the plot of that movie look like?

The exercise may seem silly, but you aren't a movie script for Walt Disney. You're writing a new script for someone much more important. You. We all love when mild-mannered Clark Kent goes into the telephone booth, changes into his costume, and proudly wears the S on his chest. The "S on your chest" needs to be the void or emptiness you feel.

How unstoppable would you be if the very thing that you previously thought held you back, now became your most significant source of strength? Combine that with the skills you already possess, learn from the misses you already made, and a new, Super You will be born.

It worked for donuts. It'll work for you. Embrace the void; make it your ally, and, little by little, you'll reshape your mind to see the opportunities that you've been previously missing.

CHAPTER 7
THE CURRENCY OF SELF-WORTH

A while back, I pondered this question: Why do some people with all the resources in the world to succeed still fail to reach their potential? Even worse, why do they limit themselves to the mediocre level of those around them when they were destined for and capable of far greater? If you're like me, you don't want to fall below your potential. To avoid that, we have to understand why most people throttle their growth.

Admittedly, I'm not an "outdoors" guy, unless I'm on a surfboard in the ocean on Waikiki Beach in Hawaii. My mom loves Hawaii as well, but perhaps the only place on Earth she loves more than Hawaii is Estes Park, Colorado. Estes Park is about an hour outside of Denver and is known for its incredible white-water rafting, wildlife, and scenic views. It's not uncommon to see massive elk, bears, and other magnificent animals. If you visit Estes Park, you'll be captivated by the seemingly endless view of the aspen trees.

The aspens grow to about 80 feet tall and in the fall, turn a magnificent shade of yellow. They grow close to each other, so from above, it looks like a sea. Though it's beautiful, there is something quite perplexing about the trees. If you look at them in Estes Park or anywhere else in the northwest, you'll notice something very peculiar. All of the trees are the same height. It's almost as if a gardener meticulously trimmed and doctored each of the thousands of eight-story trees so that no one tree rose above the other. Why is that, I asked myself.

The answer to the question of why all the aspen trees are the same height provides insight into why many of us never reach our peak form. There are two reasons that the aspen trees all grow to the same height, and all look the same. Essentially, they are the same. As an aspen tree grows, it shoots its roots out horizontally and creates new shoots that grow to become trees themselves. Since these trees are an offshoot of the first tree, each is genetically equal to the original tree. This process continues amongst the aspens in what is known as cloning.

The second reason the aspens are all the same height is that they all share the same root system. Unlike most trees that have their own roots, the aspen trees, primarily clones of one another, intertwine their powerful roots and act as one giant organism, not a plethora of individual trees. As such, since they all equally share the same resources, none of the aspens can grow above the others. Though it may have the capacity to grow much larger, because it is just one tree in a system of the aspens, it is throttled by resources being shared amongst other trees.

We've all heard the metaphor, there is strength in numbers, and while that may fundamentally be true, there is often weakness in numbers as it pertains to growth. The aspen trees are very aggressive in their growth and expansion. Their roots continue to spread wide, grow vertical, and to repeat the cycle. In doing so, the invasive root system can break up roads and sidewalks, suffocate other plant life, and even destroy the foundations of homes and buildings.

You most likely didn't pick up this book to get a botany lesson, but let's look at the similarities and implications of ourselves to the aspen. Many fall victim to a "group-think" mentality and lose their individuality. In the age of social media, algorithms are predicated on connecting like-minded people and feeding them the news and information that they want to see until that group believes the information is an undisputed truth. The problem is that, just like roots, it can become toxic for those who don't share that belief. You see it all the time in political, racial, religious, and other hot-topic discussions. A group of like minds grows and tries to force their beliefs on others, and when the others don't agree, "the roots" of the organization seek to plow through and destroy that which doesn't agree with its ideology.

While fundamentally that is an ever-growing problem, the groupthink, the aspen-tree mindset poses an even more substantial risk. What happens if the roots or source of the aspen becomes poisoned? Since the trees all rely on the same source, the poison is spread across the trees and thus risk all the aspens in that system dying.

The same happens with people. When we align ourselves with people to the point of accepting a norm and forgo thinking for ourselves and asking ourselves, "is the information or nutrients I'm receiving something that will help me grow (truth), or is this poison," we throttle our ability to grow and reach our peak potential.

This isn't a knock on surrounding yourself with a group of people with similar beliefs but rather a call on the importance of thinking for yourself so that you can make decisions and take actions that help you grow. Though you may believe you are similar to those around you, you are not a genetic clone, which means your body, mind, and soul require different nutrients. You need to be fed from a different source to reach a peak you, instead of remaining in the sea of mediocrity.

THE S-CURVE

So why is it that we don't like to go out on our own? Why is it easier to fall prey to the aspen mentality? For most of us, it's because we're not entirely sure of ourselves or our potential. Since we don't know where we're going or don't fully believe in ourselves, it's easier to just run with the pack. Sadly, the pack isn't always heading in the right direction.

How do we change that? How do we gain the courage to think for ourselves, take actions that might seemingly alienate us from the safety of the group, all with the goal of reaching our peak self? The short answer is we have to believe in ourselves and our self-worth.

You might have rolled your eyes at that last statement, trust me I cringed while writing it. Why? Because we all know believing in yourself is easier said than done, right? However, so is tying your shoe, getting up early, or eating right. Secondly, we roll our eyes because most "motivational" speakers tell you to have self-worth or live your best life. The reason I know this is because I was a part of that group the first five or six years of my speaking career. The problem isn't someone telling you to believe in yourself; in fact, we need more positive people helping lift others up. The primary fallacy of the "develop self-worth" is very few people tell you HOW.

The million-dollar question in life is "How do I believe in myself enough to step out of my comfort zone, face almost certain failure, fall on my face, get laughed at, and continue to stay on that path until I reach my goals?"

You've probably asked yourself a version of that question a hundred times. If you look at what you're asking yourself, you'll find the core of what you're asking is, "How do I know if I'm going the right way and am I sure there is a reward at the end?"

Fortunately, math shows us that you are going the right way. To believe in ourselves and start to see our worth, we have to understand the process and lifecycle of growth. In other words, we have to look at a roadmap of success so that we can identify our position, gain strength from understanding where we are, and start to be able to predict what's coming next. When we no longer fear what's next and instead adopt a mindset that allows us to look forward to what's coming, we gain confidence.

So, what is this process? In Science, it's called the Sigmoid Curve, or S-Curve for short.

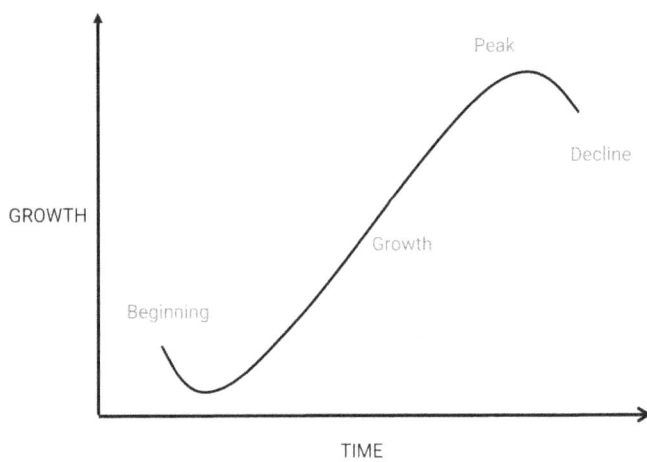

The S-curve is used by business analysts to predict the lifecycle of product sales, marketing plans, and many other metric-driven factors. What the S-curve demonstrates is that at the beginning of any new endeavor, whether that be learning a new skill, working on creating a new product, or anything in between, there is a period of perceived failure. This is commonly known as the learning curve. It's the point when it seems like nothing is working. If you've ever tried to learn a new skill or take up a new hobby, especially as an adult, you know exactly what I mean.

During this phase, nothing seems to work. Your new sales technique doesn't work; your attempt at learning a musical instrument or foreign language seems impossible. You can't get the hang of it. To start believing in ourselves, we must first understand that this phase is not only expected, but it's also necessary. When mathematicians chart the launch or growth of a plan, the data points, without fail, show this to be true.

How much different would you approach stepping out of your comfort zone if failure was expected? Remember, in the last chapter, we discussed the fallacy of perfection. What if we built on that and approached our new endeavors with a feeling of excitement every time the new attempt didn't work?

You're probably asking yourself, why would anyone approach failure with excitement? Because mathematics and the Sigmoid Curve show that after the lull, the period where nothing seems to work, if you're genuinely working at your craft, truly focusing on improvement, then the next round of data shows a period of unprecedented growth and prosperity. You get the hang of what you've been working on. You start to master the skill. Life starts to go your way. This isn't magic or luck; this is a part of the process of success.

Chances are you can identify areas of your life where you're in the lull and areas where you're in the growth. Both are important because both require growth to reach the next level, but both also give clues as to what's next.

When you're struggling and learning, you know that eventually, you'll get it, and growth will happen. In your darkest days, remind yourself that the more you work (with genuine effort and focus) on the areas that need improvement, the faster you'll reach a period of growth and prosperity. However, growth isn't the final stage because success, just like life, goes in cycles. At a certain period of prosperity, you begin to peak, plateau, and, unfortunately, decline.

Depressing huh? All that work, all that heartache, that joy of success, and then, one day, it's over. Right? Possibly – or, you could look at it differently. What if you learned to master the process of growth? I don't need to tell you how to live your life when things are going well; what we have to focus on is how we minimize the time spent in the lull, and how we start developing new skills so that we can reduce the time spent peaking or declining and instead jump right into our next stage of growth. Do you get what I'm saying? The magic of the S-curve means that instead of living a linear life of highs and lows, ups and downs, you can go through your "lull" periods while enjoying the upward trajectory of growth in other areas of your life.

DUALITY AND LEVERAGE

How do we go through the learning curve while succeeding at the same time? How do we avoid the rollercoaster of life and give ourselves the best chance of a continual upward trajectory? Is it even possible?

Successful people in business and serial entrepreneurs do it all the time. In the height of a business boom or company success, they look for ways to diversify their offerings, start new businesses, or take new chances. Mediocrity says strike while the iron is hot. Opportunity says you have to start striking before the iron even hits the fire. Many fortunes have been made, and companies saved by employing this strategy.

Perhaps the most famous example of this tactic of duality resides with visionary and entrepreneur, Elon

Musk. Musk is famous for starting Tesla Motors, Space X, the Boring Company (which is anything but boring), and a host of other major corporations with purposes that can impact humanity. His company Space X developed reusable rockets that can be deployed to the international space station, return safely, and be used again. His legendary innovations save the space program both time and money. But did you know, the now-famous Space X company, would have died had Elon not practiced duality.

Elon is famous for exploring his interests and going all-in on funding them. In the mid 90's he started a web software company and then began exploring online banking. He sold that first company, Zip2, to Compaq for hundreds of millions of dollars. Elon later founded an online bank called X.com, which would eventually become PayPal in 2000.

While PayPal was growing, Elon started exploring the thought of going to space. He had an idea to colonize Mars and to build affordable rockets. He went to Russia to meet with rocket parts suppliers to bring his idea to life. In May of 2002, he officially started his dream company, Space X. Obviously, starting a privatized Space exploration company would pose a considerable learning curve. Still, Elon used duality to start it and work out the kinks while his other businesses were on an upswing.

Later that year, PayPal was acquired for $1.5 billion, and Elon earned almost $200 million. The profits allowed him to fund Space X. Notice he didn't wait until he reached his pinnacle (the sell of PayPal), to start his next venture, he started the learning curve while the other venture was going well.

He would go on to start Tesla Motors the next year. In 2006-2008, Space X was on the brink of disaster after three failed launches. The company was running out of money and had just enough money for one last attempt at launching and landing a rocket. Again, whereas most people would cross their fingers and hope for the best, Elon was working behind the scenes.

Unbeknownst to his team at SpaceX – who believed that this last attempt was make-or-break – Elon had silently begun negotiating a $1.5B government contract with NASA, who had seen the promise and potential of SpaceX. The fourth rocket was successful; the contract was granted, and SpaceX continues to grow and improve today.

What if Elon would have waited until he peaked in each scenario? What if he would have waited to strike while the iron's hot? He would have been without money, most likely bankrupted his companies, and at the very least, would have been further behind. By employing a system of duality, working on a skill (or company) while others are on the upswing, he's been able to launch rockets, build electric cars, create solar-powered energy companies, and is currently digging tunnels underneath the United States for hyperloop transportation. This public transportation will have the capacity to transfer riders at 760 miles per hour, roughly 200 miles an hour faster than commercial airplanes.

Perhaps your goal isn't to be a billionaire, an astronaut, or make the Forbes list. Regardless of your goal, you can employ the same strategy. Take an area of your life that seems to be working in your favor. Perhaps your health and fitness are excellent, maybe you're moving up in your career, or maybe you have a great relationship. Everyone has something going in their favor. If you, for some reason, believe that nothing is going in your favor, the very fact that you have the time to sit and read this book peacefully means something in your life has to be going in your favor.

Whatever it is that is going well, ask yourself, how can I leverage the principles of what is working for me to seek out new skills or opportunities that may benefit me in the future? The beauty of leveraging a process that works for you is that you already know how to do it. You can decrease the time spent in a lull because you've already mastered a replicable process. You can take that process and apply the principles to a new skill or opportunity. By leveraging your wins, you start to set yourself on a period of continual improvement that you can celebrate without the uncertainty and shame of feeling like a failure when you're experiencing the early stages of new opportunities.

Learn to minimize the lulls in life by understanding that they are just a part of the process, and fortunately, your whole life doesn't have to be on the downswing while you're learning. You can learn and grow while you're winning in other areas of life. This process is a critical ingredient in living a life filled with opportunity and peak potential.

CHAPTER 8
YOU HAVEN'T SEEN CRAZY

In Tony Robbins' program Personal Power 2, the all-time bestselling personal development audio series, Tony says that people change for one of two reasons: (1) inspiration; or (2) desperation. While we would love to all make lifechanging alterations to our life during a spark of inspiration, many of us only make changes when we hit rock bottom.

What makes us "snap", so to speak, and get on the right track? Perhaps you have declared bankruptcy, lost a loved one, gotten a divorce, or gotten fired from your job. But what if we didn't have to hit rock bottom before we learned to harness whatever makes us "wake up"? You're probably familiar with the phrase "the elephant in the room," which is an analogy that demonstrates the subject that needs to be addressed, but no one wants to talk about it because it might make others uncomfortable. Instead of addressing the topic at hand, people tiptoe around it and whisper about it, but never address it.

But just for a second, can you imagine how the proverbial elephant feels? At some point or another, we've all been the elephant. We see those around us staring, gossiping, perhaps talking about a mistake we made or a failure we had, but knowing that they won't address us. Doesn't it infuriate you? Doesn't it make you want to snap and give people a piece of your mind?

We've all been there. Why don't we erupt? Most likely, it's for the same reason that we don't tell many people about the lofty dreams and goals we set for ourselves. We fear people calling us crazy. The lengths that most of us will go to so we can avoid being called that dreaded "C" word is remarkable. It's almost as though the designation of "crazy" puts us into an irreversible genre of people who have been banished and shunned by all of modern society.

Sounds silly doesn't it? Yet, at our core, we seek to avoid being called crazy for that very reason. But what if there is power in being crazy? What if you embraced being "the crazy" one? Now I'm not referring to the traditional meaning of crazy where you walk down the street wearing a clown suit and tuxedo shoes while mumbling to yourself and performing karate moves against the air. I'm referring to harnessing the power of crazy, or in other words, the power of extreme passion. After all, don't you want extreme results, extreme success, extreme opportunity? You can't reach crazy dreams without embracing a crazy mindset, a crazy work ethic, and thick skin to keep you from fearing being deemed crazy.

THE ARDITI

Imagine that you're a fighter pilot in an intense war, and your plane gets shot down. You are alone and separated from your allied troops by a strong enemy. You are where no one in a war wants to be; you are behind enemy lines. Perhaps you saw the movie of the same name, *Behind Enemy Lines*, loosely based on the true story of US Air Force Captain Scott O'Grady, whose plane was shot down in 1995 in the Bosnian War. For six days, he had to avoid Bosnian Serbs, who were searching for him, until the United States Marines finally rescued him. Can you imagine the stress, fear, and anxiety that being trapped behind enemy lines would create?

Now, imagine someone who is willing to land behind enemy lines. Crazy, right? That's precisely what the Italian Arditi did during the end of World War 1. The Arditi, or "Daring Ones", were a paratrooper assault special forces unit, comprised of volunteers from the Italian army. Notice that I said "volunteers". Their mission was simple: Parachute behind enemy forces, while the Italian infantry was shooting missiles at the enemy, who was bunkered down in the trenches with heavy artillery. Once they landed, they were to run through the trenches with only grenades, a dagger, and hand-to-hand combat skills, completely overtake the enemy, and then hold the bunker down for a full day before the Italian troops could arrive. It sounds like a suicide mission, doesn't it?

The Arditi's motto, "O la Vittoria, o tutti accoppati," or "We either Win or We All Die," served as the calling card of their bravery in battle. Not only were they behind enemy lines separating themselves from back up, but they also took daggers and grenades to fight against artillery shells and machine guns. Only a crazy person would do that. But the Arditi saw the benefit and logic in their craziness. They knew that in the tight trenches, there wasn't a lot of room for assault rifles and big guns. If the enemy were to try and use them, the speed of the daggers and pistols used by the Arditi would give them maneuverability and a speed advantage. The Arditi also knew that the bombardment from the Italian military mixed with the noise and chaos of throwing live grenades in bunkers gave them a distinct advantage as they were able to keep their composure while the enemy panicked.

Do you possess that mindset? Are you willing to cut yourself off from any resemblance of help or comfort zone to the point you are forced to operate with an "I win, or I die" mentality? When you cut yourself off from the safety of normalcy, you open yourself up to new possibilities. By self-creating a "desperate" situation, you can drop down into unknown trenches of war in your life with an inspired, "crazy" mentality.

You may be thinking to yourself, that's absolutely nuts. What if I tried that and failed, or got hurt, or in the case of the Arditi, died? The Daring Ones knew that in any mission, they would lose 25-30% of their troops. However, they knew the cause was even greater, and therefore, the risk was necessary. Fortunately, you're most likely not fighting in a World War, behind enemy lines, with your actual life on the line. However, we do fear the pain of failure, the growing pains of stepping out of our comfort zone, and the agony of our perceived losses. How do we combat those fears and worries?

I can't promise you that stepping out into the battlefields of life won't leave you with bruises, injuries, and scars — quite the opposite. The higher you climb and the further you grow; the harder life will hit you. The trick isn't to try and avoid every adversity that life throws at you — as that would result in returning to a fear-based comfort zone — but rather to emulate world-class boxers; learn how to take hit and roll with the punches.

PROTECT YOURSELF AT ALL TIMES

Before every professional boxing bout, the referee brings both contestants to the center of the ring and issues the instructions and rules for the fight. His final statement to the boxers is, "Protect yourself at all times." Boxing – known as the "sweet science" – is a physically demanding and violent sport. Although boxers may be great defensively and quick to avoid most punches, all boxers know that at some point in time, they will get hit – and they will get hit *hard.*

In knowing this, do you think they hope for the best, praying that their opponents' punches don't phase, stun, or knock them out? Instead, they prepare to take the punches. They practice the art of taking a hit.

Sir Isaac Newton is famous for his three laws of motion. The first law of motion states that an object in motion will remain in motion unless acted upon by another force, meaning the fist will continue to fly at a boxer until it lands on the chin, face, or body of the opponent.

The second of these irrefutable laws of motion deals with momentum in stating that the acceleration of an object is dependent upon force behind the object, aka the boxer's strength and speed. When you combine these two laws, what we find in boxing is that the stronger and faster a boxer is and the more surface area (mass) of the opposing fighter he connects with, the higher the velocity and impact will be felt by the boxer getting hit. Simply put, if a boxer hits an opponent square in the face, it will hurt more than if he doesn't hit the opponent with the full surface area of his glove.

Boxers understand that they can't control the strength or speed of their opponent. In a similar fashion, you can't control external factors in life, the adversities you face, or the hurdles life throws at you. Boxers do understand, however, that they can control how much of the opponent's glove they get with it.

Rolling with the punches is exactly what it sounds like. When a blow is aimed at the head of the boxer and it's inevitable that the punch will connect with the boxers face, the boxer will turn his head in the same direction as the punch is coming and tilt his head back so that his head goes in the same direction as the punch. This serves two purposes. A) instead of getting hit directly in the face with a fist full of leather, the boxer minimizes the surface area of his face, leaving the glove to catch a small part of his face (less mass and velocity being transferred to the face).

Secondly, by moving his head back in the same direction the punch is coming, the face isn't taking the full force of the blow because it isn't acting as a brick wall ready to absorb all the velocity. Instead, the head takes part of the force and allows the punch to stay on the same trajectory it was on.

Another way of looking at it would be if you lost control of your car and had two options. You could run directly into a brick wall head-on, or you could swerve, and the side of your car could get scraped by a concrete barrier. You know that if you hit a wall head-on, all the force and acceleration of the car would stop immediately, sending all of the energy back toward you in a catastrophic wreck. On the other hand, hitting the side of your car may still hurt, but the momentum of the vehicle isn't stopped instantly, so there is less recoil injury coming back at you to injure you.

Essentially boxers choose the path of least resistance. When a "wreck" is unavoidable, they choose not to run into that brick wall. The good news for you is that this defense system isn't naturally built into boxers. It takes years of practice to learn how to roll with the punches. Learning to take a hit is a skill. Boxers learn it's not just about assessing the oncoming punch, creating the instinct to roll with the impending blow, but they also learn to then counterattack, aka return the energy that was coming for them.

In the same manner, you have to learn how to take a hit. Boxers know that only a few potential types of "opposition" can come their way: the opponent can throw a jab (i.e., a straight punch); a hook (in which the opponent tries to hit the boxer in the side of the face or body); or an uppercut (in which the opponent tries to hit the boxer under the chin). As a result of knowing these potential attacks, they can practice rolling with the punches for each of these. In your life, perhaps you can't predict everything that may come your way, but in any industry, hobby, or venture, when you step outside your comfort zone, there's a good chance that you know the major hurdles you may face.

In a new sales role, you face the uncertainty of new clients and their potential objections. In education, you may face unruly students, parents, or bosses. In your new dieting goals, you face hunger pains, temptations, and possible headaches.

Just like boxers study the moves and tendencies of their opponent; you, too, can dissect the potential attacks of the area in which you wish to seek and find opportunities in your life. Prepare yourself to land in the trenches; train your mind to find calm in the chaos; learn to roll with the punches and be prepared to attack with a smile on your face. When they tell you that you're crazy, tell them, "You ain't seen nothing yet!"

CHAPTER 9
THE NUMBERS GAME

Years ago, I left the country for the first time. On a whim, my sister and I decided that we would visit the Incan Ruins at Machu Pichu in Peru because she saw a picture of the ruins on the cover of a travel book at a bookstore. My sister is a world traveler, so international flights and new cultures are second-nature to her. However, this was my first foray outside the comfort of the English-speaking United States, and it was a complete shock to me. The second we landed at the airport, I realized how out of place I was. Everything was in Spanish; virtually no one spoke any English, and everything seemed the opposite of how it was in the United States.

I knew going into the trip that Peru didn't use US dollars and that I'd have to get my money transferred into Peruvian Sols, the currency of Peru. I didn't put much more thought into it other than that. However, a strange thing happened when I got my Peruvian money. I handed my US dollars to the currency converter, and to my surprise, the Peruvian money she gave me back was almost four times as much as the dollars I gave her. For a second I thought that she messed up and I had got lucky. Then it hit me. Money isn't worth the same everywhere. $100 in America will get me $100 worth of goods. That same $100 in buying power in Peru will get me the equivalent of $400 worth of goods and services.

What changed? Did I do something magical? Was it because I was special? No, the currency rates changed because of my location, and the value of what I had increased solely for that reason. Several investors make a living trading currency on the Foreign Exchange (forex) market, whereby they buy money in certain currencies, wait until the exchange rates are favorable in another country, and sell them there. Can you believe that? You can make money just by moving your existing money to a different area.

Where am I going with this? Life works the same way. So many times, because of the circumstance we're in, the job we have, the circle of friends and family around us, we don't see our real value. Because of where we are, we don't see our worth. If only we were to move ourselves to a different area, aka find a favorable exchange rate for our skills, we could immediately increase our perceived value. Notice I didn't say real value, because you're not worth less just because others don't see it. However, we all want to be valued at the highest level of our worth. That goes for business, relationships, friendships, and other aspects of life.

Now I'm not suggesting that you move to a foreign country in hopes they sing your praises, but rather to look at the areas of life you're complacent or comfortable in and ask yourself this, "am I maximizing my value or am I valued at the highest standard possible while in this environment?" It's human nature to start taking people and situations for granted when they are a part of your routine. To your friends, perhaps you're the one they depend on for advice, but would happen if you went to the market and charged a premium to businesses for that same advice as a consultant?

Don't think it's possible? I made a living doing that very same thing. The bulk of the suggestions that I provide when I consult with clients comes from the same conversations that I have with friends. The reason is that, underneath the job titles, socioeconomic differences, and company logos, we are all just people trying to figure out who we are or where we're going. It's that simple. The trick to putting yourself in the position of being valued (and to presenting opportunities for yourself) is to look at your skillset and ask yourself, "How can I take this skill and help people: (a) figure out who or where they are; or (b) help people get where they want to go?" Any profession can be the answer to one of those two questions, so you aren't limited to being a business consultant or entrepreneur.

By understanding which of those two questions you can solve for someone, the more focused you can become in prospecting where you should position yourself in the currency exchange of life to receive maximum value for your services. This isn't just related to money either. Not everyone views opportunity as monetary or status gain. A friend of mine is one of those people who loves to love people. The problem is she hangs around a group of us that are more into discussing the next business move and company to start than we are into sitting around, hugging and expressing our feelings. Of course, we value her kind heart, but I'm sure to some degree we take her for granted. However, using this method of finding a currency exchange that will give her the value she deserves, she recently began visiting widows and widowers in nursing homes across the city. She said she feels genuine joy as the eyes of the patrons she visits light up when she enters their rooms, gives them great big hugs, and sits for hours visiting about the weather, grandkids, soap operas, and more.

She found her opportunity by knowing what she had to offer and then figuring out where that service would be valued the highest. For her, the reward was love, smiles, and knowing she made a difference. Another friend of mine is an avid duck hunter. He visits the lakes and swamps of Louisiana to hunt ducks and other birds. I asked him why he doesn't hunt duck around Dallas, to which he replied, "because there are no ducks to hunt here." As simple as that answer may seem, it's profound when it comes to opportunity. You see, he might be equipped to hunt ducks in Dallas, but if there aren't any, then all the skill, weapons, and hunting apparel mean nothing. But by moving himself into an area that has what he's after, he's able to execute on what he's good at. The travesty of life is that so many don't see their worth because they're standing in the wrong area waiting for the right opportunity.

There's an opportunity out there for each of us. It's up to us to figure out what it is we have to offer. Don't worry if you don't know what you have to offer. I'll give you the guide to figuring that out in upcoming chapters. For now, you have to start deciding where you can position yourself to get the maximum value for your time, energy, and skills.

110% IS A LIE

As a Wide Receiver on the Baylor University football team, I remember sitting in the pre-game meetings and listen to our coach tell us to "go out there and give 110%". I used to laugh at how ridiculous that sounded – someone wanting more effort from you than you have the capacity to give. Yet in locker rooms, classrooms, and boardrooms across the world, leaders ask the same thing from their teams: "Give 110%." There's one fundamental flaw in that logic. You can't give more than you have. If I gave you a gallon of water and told you, "I want you to use that one water jug and fill a two-gallon bucket without refilling the jug," would you be able to do it? No, because you only have one gallon to start with.

You can't give more than you have, and you can't operate at a higher level than your maximum effort. At the end of the day, 100% is the maximum you can give in any situation. It's important to understand this principle because life force-feeds this "110%" lie to us and often leaves us feeling inferior, as though we're not giving our all, or that even though we're giving our all, we are still inadequate. That's a dangerous game to play with our minds and careers. Even more so, think about the vehicle you drive. What would happen if you pushed the pedal to the metal and forced the engine to operate at 100% with the goal of trying to push it to 110% of its capacity? First, you can't go faster than the car can go; secondly, if you push it to the max for too long, you'll blow out the engine.

If you're constantly burning both ends of the candle in life, hustling to give 110%, you WILL burn out. It's inevitable. Not only that, you'll feel like a failure for not being able to reach the coveted 110%. You're being set up for failure by attempting to give more than you have.

You're probably thinking, this is the complete opposite of inspirational, that is until you look at what we CAN do. None of us are capable of giving more than we have to give, but there are two upsides. First, almost all of us stop far short of what we believe our 100% is. Retired Navy Seal David Goggins said that when you reach your absolute physical limits, you're only 40% of what you're actually capable of pushing yourself to. Muhammad Ali was once asked how many pushups he did per day. He said he didn't have the answer because he didn't even start counting until he got tired.

The point is you haven't reached 100%, but there's even better news. We don't have to focus on reaching 100% as much as we need to focus on something far more important, increasing our capacity. Ali knew that if he just focused on getting better at the same number of pushups per day, let's say 1000, then he would only become great at doing 1000 pushups. For most of us, that would be 100% we are happy with. We often get a number or figure or defining metric in our head and say, this is the 100%. Though your capable of far more, your mind says, "okay, I'll limit myself to make that the ceiling at which I'm capable." Ali, one of the greatest champions in the history of boxing, didn't want to fall into that paradox. He knew that if he only counted when he was tired, then over time he was he wasn't just doing 1000 pushups, he was doing 1000 pushups on top of however many his previous limit was, thus increasing his strength capacity by operating on that sliding scale.

Do you remember earlier when I asked you to fill a two-gallon bucket with a one-gallon jug? We know that's impossible, but what if I gave you a two-gallon jug and asked you to do the same thing? You'd be able to because the capacity of what you are pouring from is greater than it was. In a similar fashion, when you focus on increasing your capacity, you improve your ability to get desired results. A Lamborghini starts faster and goes faster than a motorized scooter. Why? The engine capacity is much larger and propels the vehicle at a higher rate. The Lamborghini wouldn't have to give 100% effort to beat the scooter no matter how hard the scooter tried.

Many of us go through life by trying to get the most out of our "scooter", instead of asking ourselves how we can increase our capacity — or, in the case of vehicles, increase our horsepower — so that we can perform more efficiently, quicker, and with less effort. But how do we harness a mindset like Ali's, Goggins', and that of a host of other champions and heroes? We must start by not limiting our capacity to imaginary, finite numbers and start operating on a growth scale for percentile improvement.

THE PERCENTAGE THEORY

In Chapter One, we uncovered the realization that we lie to ourselves often. Up to a point, it's good to realize that because we open ourselves to the possibility of change. However, to home in on an opportunity, we have to do more than realize. We have to shift towards change.

I'll admit it can be hard to break a habit. It can be hard to seek a new you or seek genuine change when you're stuck in a mental cycle predicated on a past lie that you believed to be true. I see this most often when I speak to companies' sales departments. Many times, a company will ask me to speak to low performing salesmen, and without fail, in every company, the reason for the low performance of at least one salesman is the lies they tell themselves.

I start with a simple question, how's it going this month? The response (and lie) is, "oh, it's going pretty good." I used to look at their numbers, which clearly indicate otherwise and stand there baffled. Was this person delusional? Do they think they are superior in intellect and can fool me with eloquent words? For years I tried to help them see things from their superior's point of view. We'd try techniques, new strategies, bonus plans, and a plethora of other ideas. For some reason, nothing seemed to work for that type of sales employee.

One day it hit me, the same reason that that people lie to themselves about their job performance is the same reason people lie about their progress in weight loss, lie about their progress in their financial goals and other aspects of life. The reason is, they don't realize they're lying. Not that they don't realize they aren't where they are supposed to be, they've just conditioned their mind to think they can make it up later, or they find a subjective past event to compare their current performance too, a la, I am behind on my goal to lose 30 pounds in 6 months, but I'm not as heavy as I was three months ago, so I'm doing "pretty good."

I hate the "pretty good" lie. We all tell it to ourselves in some aspect. As a result, I tested a theory with various salesman and those trying to lose weight and encouraged managers at companies I speak at to try it with their teams.

The theory is simple. When assessing performance, get input from the performer on his/her perceived performance capacity, pair that with a finite timeframe, and evaluate performance at defined times with percentages only.

Performance Capacity + Time Frame + Assessment via Percentages = INABILITY TO LIE

Let's illustrate it this way: A low-performing salesman's company would like him to sell 20 cars per month; however, he hasn't sold more than 10 per month for the last six months. With the percentage theory, the manager would sit down with the salesman and ask, "How many cars are you capable of selling next month?" Without fail, when given the option to contribute to their metrics, a performer will give an answer above what they have been producing. The importance of getting their input is allowing them to set the standard for what they can sell, and thus removing the "Y'all ask too much of me" excuse that many use. Secondly, it develops a rapport with the performer by allowing them to contribute to their growth. It gives the illusion of shared responsibility.

Now let's say the performer said they know they can sell 15 cars next month, though the history has shown that most likely isn't true, it's not important. What's important is they set the performance metric for themselves.

Next, you create agreed-upon designated days to assess performance. Perhaps on the 10th of the month, the 20th of the month, and at the end. During these assessment checkups, you speak only in percentages. IF the goal is 15 cars sold in the month, a standard set by the employee, then by the meeting on the 10th they should have sold five cars. Rather than saying, "you've only sold three cars, you have to pick it up," you simply say, "you're performing at 60% of what you said you're capable of, you're failing."

NO ONE wants to fall below a standard they set for themselves. By breaking the process down into digestible timeframes and assessing performance based on the percentage they should be at for that current timeline, you eliminate the standard excuses and delusions of "making it up at the end of the month." Notice I said to speak about the percentages based on where they should be at that point in the month. If on the 10th, the manager would have said, you've sold three cars and you have to sell 15 this month, you're operating at 20% capacity, the salesman might as well give up, it seems impossible to recover.

By keeping them accountable based on percentages as an assessment of performance in a given period with feedback from the employee, the performer is unable to continue the cycle of self lies. This works in sales and any aspect that you can measure progress. You can apply it to weight loss, savings, and any other metric in your life.

To shift our mindsets away from how we used to be and to find freedom in who we may become, we have to trap the lies and excuses we've been accustomed to feeding ourselves with. By forcing ourselves to look at our performance based on where we should be based on the goals we set for ourselves, we are forced to see the hard truths of our performance, for better or worse.

If you're falling below your potential — even though you're giving you're all — then rest assured; I'll help you sharpen your skillset in the next section of this book to increase your capacity and help you improve your performance.

SHARPEN

*"It is possible to fly without motors,
but not without knowledge or skill."*
-Wilbur Wright

CHAPTER 10
BUILDING THE
OPPORTUNITY WINDOW

If you've made it this far in our journey together, then you've undoubtedly asked yourself some difficult questions, found areas where you have limited yourself, and begun to shift your perspective to see new opportunities. While we could immediately go chase opportunities now, there's a step we can take that will allow us to pursue, find, or create opportunities more effectively. That step is to build upon the mental shifts we made and sharpen our skills.

You might be thinking the question that many of us do when we are inspired to take any action but held back for some reason or another, "what if I miss my opportunity?" There is, perhaps, a chance of missing an opportunity, because in my years of research in studying opportunity, I've learned that specific opportunities often have an expiration date. Do you know what else I've learned in my research? Chasing great opportunities, while ill-equipped, is the equivalent of chasing a cheetah through the African landscape. You can do your best, but unless something happens to the cheetah, you aren't going to catch it.

We all miss opportunities. The new goal is to prevent falling victim to the ideology of a "window of opportunity," which suggests that you have to be In the right place at the right time, with the right circumstances, to have a chance at capitalizing on the opportunity you want. As an opportunity engineer, you don't leave your fate to luck, chance, or being in the right place by accident. What we have to do is shift from a mindset of chasing a fleeting window of opportunity and instead look deep inside ourselves and realize, we have the tools to build the opportunity window.

Do you see the difference? A window of opportunity means it's out of your control, and your good fortune is dependent on many other factors, none of which you can influence. Building the opportunity window demonstrates that if you use your toolset or skills, which I call "Opportunity Finders," you can create the platform that allows you to spot and capitalize on opportunities with much higher frequency and efficiency.

The difference in the window of opportunity versus building the opportunity window is the equivalent of staring into the night sky at the stars and planets with your bare eyes versus viewing the same planets and stars with the Hubble Space Telescope.

The Hubble Telescope is a gigantic solar-powered 43.5-foot telescope that orbits around the Earth once every 95 minutes. Since its launch in 1990, the orbiting telescope has discovered stars and galaxies, new moons on planets, and has provided insights into season and weather patterns on planets in our solar system because of its high-powered cameras and imaging systems.

For a few weeks in July, the average person on Earth can look into the night sky and see what appears to be a star but is the planet Saturn. Available only to the naked eye for those few weeks once a year, the viewing of Saturn has a small window of opportunity.

However, astronomists and researchers built the Hubble Space Telescope with the expressed goal of studying the universe. Because of the powerful telescope, and its position in space, not only can the Hubble Telescope see Saturn for a far greater window of time than the naked eye; it can also see Saturn with remarkable accuracy. The telescope captured pictures of many of Saturn's moons, as well as the hexagonal pattern formed around Saturn's North Pole. By building the "opportunity window" with the telescope, scientists created more opportunities to study the ringed planet and to explore the planet and other galaxies in immense detail.

Which would you rather do? View the stars with the naked eye at a time only the stars grant you or create the mechanism by which you can view the stars as often as you want in as much depth as you want? To find opportunity, you have to ask yourself, "what are tools I have that I can build upon and enhance to see opportunities on a larger and more in-depth scale?" You can create your own window, by which you control opportunity instead of being a passenger on the "I'll show up when I want to" opportunities that many fall prey into waiting for.

But how? How do we develop our toolset to build a powerful telescope or window to discover new opportunities? We first must find out who we are at our core.

MOUNTAIN GOATS KNOW BEST

Ten thousand feet above sea level in the Rocky Mountains, mountain goats stand perched against vertical cliffs. As an outsider looking at the goats, it's natural to think, "are they crazy?" What if they fall? Are they stuck? From an outsider's view, it looks like the mountain goats are in a world of trouble. Thankfully, the mountain goats don't gage danger or difficulty from the viewpoint of others. This is because mountain goats know what they're made of – they know their foundation. Mountain goats have a unique hoof comprised of a hard outside to grip the rocks. The inside of their hooves is soft, creating a non-slip surface to give the goats added traction on the slippery rocks. With only two inches of surface area, a mountain goat can lift and balance its entire body. Where the rest of the world sees danger, the mountain goats find safety.

They know that high on the sides of cliffs and mountains, predators cannot reach them.

What are you made of? What is your foundation? What is it about you that gives you an advantage in an area of life other people fear? To begin to find opportunity, we have to find our footing, so to speak.

Think about the last time you turned the lights off in a room and everything seemed pitch-black. You probably experienced this last night when you got in bed. At first, you can't see anything, but after a few minutes, what happens? Your eyes start to adjust, because your pupils dilate to let in more light, and you can begin to make out objects in the room. Essentially, you are able to see in the dark. Why weren't you immediately able to see in the dark when the lights were first turned off? You had the ability, didn't you? Your eyes know how to see in the dark, the only difference is, they were yet conditioned to adapt to the change of scenery.

But they are capable. We're all capable of far more than we realize, we have to let our eyes "adjust to the dark." The unfamiliarity of pursuing a new goal can blind us with fear, but just like a dark room, if we're willing to trust ourselves, we will find a way to adjust and see the light. Opportunity favors those who are willing to look in the dark.

Night vision goggles allow our armed forces to perform stealthy nighttime missions by giving them the ability to see clearly in pitch-black enemy environments. Night vision works in a similar fashion as your pupils dilating to allow more light in, so you can see in the dark. The difference between the human eye's ability to see at night, and the night vision goggles' ability is that night vision goggles take the light and electronically amplifies it to give the eye a clearer view. Likewise, if you want to find immense opportunity, you have to look for your opportunity finders, and then figure out how you can amplify those skills or traits.

Are you an extroverted person who's convincing and good with people? Perhaps you already know that you might perform well in a sales role because you have a gift with influencing people. Understanding that gift is the first step, but how then can you amplify that skill to see new opportunities? We'll get into the process of amplifying those talents in the next few chapters, but for now, let's look at what sets us apart from others.

The mountain goats' competitive advantage is its hooves and ability to balance on cliffs. Cats, lions, and other felines have the advantage of stealth paws that make virtually no noise and allow them to sneak up on prey. We don't have to be wild animals to possess a competitive advantage foundation. We need only ask ourselves what is it that we do better than anyone around us. Opportunity isn't about having to be the best in the world at a task. It's often about being better than those around you that are competing for the same opportunity.

Perhaps it's your personality, some trait that others deem "weird," perhaps it's a relentless mindset or some obscure talent or gift. Maybe it's your ability to network and connect with people, your patience in being able to listen and give advice, or maybe you have a knack for spotting typos and grammar errors in essays better than anyone around you (as is the case with my editor.) In any scenario, the first step toward sharpening our toolset to start identifying opportunities is to locate that foundation in ourselves.

Think about it for a second. There is something about you that you do better than anyone else. If not better, what is it about you that you do differently than anyone else? Opportunity often goes against conventional wisdom and the status quo.

THE RED PANDA

Standing at a mere five feet tall, the Chinese born Rong Niu might not stand out in a crowd on the street. Rong, a fourth-generation acrobat just like her mother, grandmother, and great grandmother before her is a bowl flipper. This is a common acrobatic move in China where acrobats often flip bowls from their feet or hands onto the heads of their counterparts. However, at the age of seven, Rong's dad realized something special about his daughter. Whereas most people worked in teams and flipped bowls on to each other's heads, young Rong was able to balance and flip bowls from her feet onto her head with remarkable accuracy. Though bowl flipping was common amongst acrobats, doing so solo stood out.

After she mastered bowl flipping, she began experimenting with flipping bowls while riding on a unicycle, a one-wheeled bicycle. After a stint on America's Got Talent, the sports world became obsessed with her. Though she may not stand out in a crowd, when Rong climbs aboard her 8 foot tall, $25,000 unicycle, she transforms into her stage-name — the Red Panda — and performs her routine to the thunderous applause of sellout crowds at halftime shows in the NBA and other sporting events around the world.

The foundation was the ability to flip bowls on her head. The unicycle was the amplification of that foundation. As she continued to hone her craft, she started riding taller unicycles, leading to further amplification. As unorthodox as it seems, the Red Panda found what worked for her and has made a legendary career out of it. Her show is so mesmerizing that she continually ranks as one of the top halftime acts in professional sports.

You have a unique skill. You have a different talent. It's time to set that talent as the cornerstone upon which you'll build your opportunity window for the remainder of this book and beyond.

CHAPTER 11
DIG DEEP AND DOUBLE-DOWN

Rich Mendoza, an accomplished entrepreneur and great friend of mine, has a beautiful Presidential Rolex watch. I've seen some exquisite timepieces in my day, but his gold Rolex is a statement piece. Anytime we're out, people comment on the watch. Over the last year or so, I've made note of an interesting fact: Although he offers people fantastic advice on their business ventures – advice that, if taken, could allow people to build their own businesses and purchase their own Rolex – they would rather sit and remain fascinated by Rich's watch instead.

Even worse, they comment on the beauty of the watch and then go on about their day. I'm not that kind of person. You aren't either. There are two types of people in the world. Those that look at something of high value, such as a Rolex and say, "wow, that's nice" and move on without much more thought than that, and there's the second group of people, you and me. We look at a high dollar timepiece, or successful business and say, "that's nice, but how does it work? What makes it so valuable?"

One of the major keys to positioning yourself to find opportunity is to ask yourself the question, "what are the building blocks upon which success is built?" By focusing on those building blocks, you find ample ways to improve because you begin to realize that success isn't linear. Ultra-successful people look at their foundational skillset and then break it down and figure out what the building blocks of that skill are. In doing so, they always find something they can improve upon.

One of the main reasons a Rolex watch is worth so much is that it isn't battery-powered, and the second-hand doesn't tick around the face of the bezel, but rather moves in a smooth, continual circle around the watch. Because it isn't battery-powered, the Rolex will perpetually last forever.

The reason it's able to do this is that the inside of the watch boasts an intricate system called Perpetual Movement made up of over 220 parts, compared to the 50 parts inside most watches that take the watchmaker a year to make. Only certified Rolex dealers have the tools to be able to open and look inside the famed timepiece.

The goal of living a fulfilled life is not to have incremental success, like the ticking second hand of a regular watch, but to enjoy perpetual growth and achievement like a Rolex. In the same fashion, we must look deep inside ourselves at our skillset and beg the question, "It's good, but how does it work?" What are the pieces? How can I improve upon what I'm already great at?

In the last chapter, we discussed the cornerstone skill that we will use to find opportunities throughout this book. Look at that skill, or opportunity finder, right now, and write down what are the building blocks that make you good at that skill. The reason for this is by doing so, you find several areas you can focus on to improve that will ultimately help your grand skill become more effective; you are sharpening the ax that you will use to cut hack away at the tree of opportunity.

Due to having 220 internal parts, a Rolex maker can analyze each of those pieces to see if any can be improved. If a piece is improved, then it makes the entire watch better. Your career is no different. If you can improve upon an aspect, then the whole of who you are will also improve.

Rich, for instance, owns a mega factory creating every type of garment, athletic uniform, apparel, or high-scale print job imaginable. It's easy to walk into the large showroom displaying his company, XSports, capability, and see all the employees bustling around in their various roles and think, wow, this is a big company. However, keeping in line with asking how it works, it's interesting to realize that only five or six years ago, Rich started with a basic T-shirt screen printing press. He printed some great shirts, but rather than tell himself he was a good T-shirt printer, he looked at his cornerstone skillset, which was that he had a knack for apparel and knowing what it was that people wanted to wear. First, he flew to China to learn the print trade firsthand. He doubled down on that skillset. Then he began to try different types of printing to get the desired results he wanted, vinyl, sublimation, and more. He added an embroidery aspect. After that, he hired great seamstresses with immense knowledge to be able to offer cut & sew garments and athletic uniforms.

Every time he reached a new level in printing, he doubled down and found the best people to improve that aspect of the business, and he looked at a different cog of the company and found ways to expand offerings or improve current ones.

As a result, six years later, his mega factory can create virtually any type of print or apparel in-house at a turnaround time that's unbeatable. The point is, Rich knew his skill was his vision for apparel, he didn't limit himself to an aspect of printing. Too often, we become myopic in what we believe our foundational skill is and therefore miss out on opportunities to double down, look at the building blocks, and find cogs in those building blocks of our careers and talents that allow us room to grow.

What was your foundational skill from the previous chapter? What are the building blocks? The more pieces you can break your skill down in to, the more opportunity you will have for growth, and ultimately the more opportunities your skill will present you with.

If you're struggling with identifying yours, don't worry, I struggled too. Early in my career, I thought my skill was speaking. Ten years ago, If I would have read this book and completed this exercise, I would have looked at the building blocks behind speaking and built from there. Though that wouldn't have been a bad skill to focus on, I would have missed a lot of opportunity, why? Because though speaking is what I believed my gift was, the actual cornerstone of my skillset was putting words together, a wordsmith.

I don't say that to come across as someone who has mastered language or reached the pinnacle of prose, but instead to help you look at the skill you think you have and ask yourself, yes that may be an aspect of my skill, but is it the ABSOLUTE foundation? The deeper you can dig, the higher you can grow.

By focusing on being a wordsmith, I found more opportunities to grow. As an author, there are many building blocks that I continually work on: thought cohesiveness, the ability to illustrate a point, sentence structure, readability, and entertainment value. Improving each of these aspects helps the entire foundation of wordsmithing, much like enhancing any area of your home improves the overall value of the house. As a speaker, I look at the building blocks of storytelling: tonality, annunciation, humor, pauses, escalating and de-escalating energy for added impact, and a host of other individual blocks that make up the entity of speaking, which again helps the overall foundation that I've built on words.

Look at your skill again. Is it truly the foundation? Now, don't get so caught up in worrying about not having your core foundation that you don't even start improving yourself but be mindful when creating your list of building blocks and working on improving them that there may be something deeper. If you find a deeper foundation while working on your skill, it's okay. Those are still aspects of the foundation, so your time hasn't been wasted. If anything, the focus you've given to that aspect of your skill will help you create opportunities much quicker.

But we must dig deep. That phrase often made me roll my eyes as much as the "you have to have self-worth" phrase, because what does it mean? Perhaps the best instance of how to dig deep and why we should was found beginning in the 7th century in Feudal Japan.

SAMURAIS AND THE KATANA BLADE

Samurai Warriors, a member of the elite social and military class in ancient and premodern Japan, were noble warriors. Bound by a code of honor, or Bushido, the legendary warriors devoted their lives to justice, benevolence, courage, honor, politeness, loyalty, and sincerity. Sworn to defend their masters and family, these warriors were easy to spot. Why? Because Samurai warriors never parted from their swords.

The fabled sword known as the Katana Blade, made famous by their depiction in television and movies, was a single-edged curved blade sword. From the age of 7, young Samurais began learning to use the famed blade. They learned how to strike, where to strike, the importance of the blade, and the responsibility that came with it. The swords were so revered that when a young Samurai was being born, a sword was brought into the bedchambers. When a Samurai lay on his deathbed, his sword accompanied him to protect him for one last fight. The Katanas were passed from father to son. The Japanese placed so much reverence on the swords that Priests were often called in during the creation of the sword to bless the Katana Blade.

Why were these swords so valuable? Why did Samurais keep the sword by their side always? It wasn't just about protection, rank, admiration, or habit. The Samurai warriors took such good care of their swords because the swords not only represented Japan, they represented the Soul of the Samurai. Yes, Samurai, believed the soul of who they were was contained in that noble blade.

Think about that for a second, imagine the skill we've been discussing the last few chapters as a sharp blade that you will use to attack the opportunities you find in life. How much more pride, energy, and time would you put into perfecting that craft if the soul of your existence laid in that skill?

Guess what? It does. Whether or not you realize it; what you do, how you act, and the people you interact with and admire are a representation of you. In every situation, you're creating a legacy and leaving a mark on society, on your loved ones, and on your circle. The question you must ask yourself is: "What kind of legacy am I leaving? Am I sharpening my blade, skills, and gifts so that I'll be precise, noble, and live a life that others admire and respect? Or am I going through life haphazardly with a dull blade and leaving the mark of mediocrity on those I touch because I didn't value the soul of my existence enough to sharpen my skill?

The reason Samurais are legendary is that they lived their lives with a code of ethics — and the soul of that code and their being was in that blade. Every day, as you continue to build upon your foundation, you are forging the sword of opportunity for your life. You'll use it to defend yourself against those who seek to destroy your opportunities, and you'll use it to carve a path of opportunity for yourself and your loved ones.

Do you want to risk fighting this battle with a dull blade? Isn't it time to not only sharpen the blade and improve upon those building blocks of your foundation so that you can win the battle for your dreams, goals, and future?

The Samurais did it. Ultra-successful people sharpen their blade daily, and now, so will you.

CHAPTER 12
DO LESS, ACCOMPLISH MORE

Bruce Lee, the famed martial artist and actor, was credited with creating his own style of martial arts. Unimpressed with the traditional method of martial arts, which he felt weren't realistic in real-world scenarios, he created Jeet Kun Do, the way of the intercepting fist. Lee referred to Jeet Kun Do as "the style with no style", as it didn't place emphasis on any movements or traditional moves but instead stressed the importance of fluidity, speed, and formlessness. Lee's goal was to fight like water, which is formless and shapeless and can adapt to any vessel.

The main goal of Jeet Kun Do was to provide advocates a manner to use minimal effort and gain maximum results. There was no clearer illustration of the power in this philosophy than Bruce Lee's coined "one-inch punch." The punch, exactly like its namesake, allowed Bruce Lee to start with his fist one inch from an opponent, yet enabled him to generate enough force to lift an opponent off their feet and drive them backward. What's even more impressive is that Bruce Lee wasn't the size of someone like heavyweight boxing champion Mike

Tyson, but rather a 5'8, 128 lb. man. The one-inch punch wasn't just a dramatic movie-special effects move, but a move that has been analyzed, vetted and emulated by others.

There are two main reasons Lee can pull off this punch. First and foremost, he practices the punch. Bruce famously said, "it's far better to fear a man who practices one kick a thousand times than a man who practices one thousand kicks, one time." In terms of opportunity, we must adopt this mindset of focusing on what our skills and related skills are. Too often, we diversify far too quickly and never gain mastery of anything. While it is vital to develop the skills, or building blocks, inside our craft, we must be sure we are building upon a foundation to grow instead of spreading wide and thin in ways that make us lose focus on our cornerstone skill.

The second reason Bruce Lee can generate so much force in one inch that he can lift an opponent off the ground is that he isn't just using his fist. Though the move is quick and precise, biomechanical researchers at Stanford University observed that Lee used his entire body, starting with his legs, hip turn, shoulders, arm, and finally, the fist. Though the actual "punch" is one inch of movement, force and velocity are generated by his entire body.

To find opportunity, we must employ the same concept. Use everything deep inside ourselves, driven toward one "contact point" with all of force, energy, and might. Again, easier said than done. So, what are we saying since the odds are most of us aren't experienced martial artists who can break concrete slabs with our bare hands? What we're saying is focus. Not only is finding opportunity about focusing on the opportunity, but it's also about focusing on accomplishing more by doing less.

Conventional wisdom says that to knock an opponent out with a punch, you need to rear back as far as you can to generate speed and deliver the most forceful punch possible. Brue Lee realized it was more about focused, quality movement, not quantity movement. Why spend the unnecessary time and energy, when you could get better results faster and with less energy? Which would you rather do?

IT'S COMPLICATED

If you've been following along in this book, then by now, you probably have a good idea of what the skill (i.e., opportunity finder) that you're seeking to develop to find opportunities is. But how can we make it more efficient? How can we generate the same or better opportunities with less effort and still get the results we want? It starts by analyzing our process.

When you think about the process you take to get a result, whether that's to close deals and make money, lose weight and gain muscle, or even socially trying to find a partner or future spouse, what do you do? Let's start by writing down the actual process we believe that we take to get to the intended result that we want.

Mary Barra, CEO of General Motors, did precisely that. In 2014, her first year of being CEO, GM recorded record numbers despite a disaster that forced General

Motors to recall 30 million vehicles. To stand in the face of disaster and lead your global organization to record numbers, the company had to do something innovative, right?

At the 2015 Catalyst Awards, Mary was asked what innovative changes she made to turn the company around that quickly. Her response wasn't anything you'd expect. Most would think she created a new vehicle, improved technology, delivered a great marketing plan, or improved incentives or something to that degree. However, Barra said perhaps the most innovative change she made at GM had to do with the employee dress code in what she called "the smallest big change."

She analyzed the GM dress code, which was ten pages long and covered every aspect of dress for everyone from salespeople, to C-level execs, down to the assembly line and engineers. With so many roles in the 200,000+ people that General Motors employees and with so many cultural standards to account for in the 140 countries that GM serves and operates in, Mary thought the dress code was too complicated. After all, isn't "no t-shirts with writing on it that can be misinterpreted" too vague? Just as beauty is in the eye of the beholder, so too is the opportunity to misunderstand.

Mary made a drastic change that sent shockwaves through the company. She scrapped the ten-page dress code and replaced it with two words. "Dress Appropriately." There was no fine print, no clauses or subpoints. The entire enterprise would now abide by those two words, "dress appropriately."

A fundamental reason this new dress code was successful is that it was easy to understand, and it empowered the managers themselves to be responsible for their teams versus having every nuance of a mandated infraction run through Human Resources, saving time and money.

Some managers complained originally stating that some of their employees dress too skimpy." Mary responded. "No amount of dress code rules will fix that behavior. It's up to you to become a leader." Little by little, managers and teams came up with levels of appropriateness that worked for their teams. For instance, one group settled on allowing its teams to wear jeans to work just if they kept a pair of dress pants at their desks in case of an important impromptu meeting.

By stripping away pages of red tape, rules, and limiting parameters, Mary was able to look at what the overall goal of a dress code was and integrate it at its most efficient core. Remember, the way to clear up any process is often to remove, never to add pieces. Doctors remove the blockage in veins to allow blood flow to and from the heart more efficiently. Plumbers remove clogged pipes to allow water to drain. You must ask yourself, "What can I remove from my process to get results quicker?"

A friend of mine works as a sales manager for a large company, and as I visited his office one day, I noticed him taking a significant amount of time copying numbers from various screens, pasting them in different spreadsheets on another screen and then taking those numbers and inputting them in a third spreadsheet. Sitting there puzzled at the work it took to create one quote as his employee stood there waiting, and knowing that Excel spreadsheets have functions you can build to auto-populate all that data for you, I asked him, "why do you do all those steps when you could set the formulas and have it all done on one screen instantly?" He said, "I don't know. This is just how we've always done it."

We're all guilty of it. We all have areas of our lives we need to clean up. If you're struggling to find ways to clean up your process so that you can start to find opportunity, ask yourself this. What is the intended goal of the process? Besides each step of the process, you wrote down ask yourself this. Is this step Critical to get to the intended result? The reasoning behind this is that often, we put band-aids on problems as temporary fixes, always telling ourselves that we'll fix it later, and over time it just becomes the norm. We only accept the pieced-together process as our new method of operation, with little thought as to why we do it.

We must clear these traffic jams in our process that our disabling us from reaching our potential quicker. We must do less in order to focus more. We need one-inch punches that win the fight, not long winding uppercuts that have a high rate of missing our target.

Case in point, my brother played football at Texas Tech under legendary head coach Mike Leach. Coach Leach is known for his off the wall interviews on topics ranging from pirates, bigfoot, aliens, tracking raccoons, and a litany of other memorable interviews. Google "Mike Leach Interviews," and you'll laugh for hours. To get an idea of the kind of guy he is, in addition to his current role as the head football coach at Washington

State University, he also decided he'd like to teach a class at the University. The class, which is so popular than an application essay must be written to have a chance at being selected, is named "insurgent warfare and football strategy."

As intriguing of a character as he is off the field, on the field, he's known for something greater. Leach is well known across the country for his record-setting offenses and his ability to put a lot of points on the scoreboard very quickly.

What's more impressive is that he accomplishes this feat by doing the opposite of what "conventional wisdom" says to do. On most teams, the offensive line — the five big guys in the middle whose job it is to block for the running back or block to give the quarterback enough time to throw the ball down the field — are usually close together to prevent defenders from going between them. Leach does the opposite; he spreads them out. As a result, the defense must spread out, too, creating space for his running back. Most teams value a statistic called "time of possession," which is the amount of time that a team's offense has the ball. The logic is if our team has the ball, the other team can't score. In an interview after a victory over a rival, Leach was asked about the discrepancy in time of possession, since his team had the ball for about 1/4 of the amount of time as the opponent. Leach responded, "*Time of possession is the most overrated statistic in football.*"

Leach said this because he knew what his goal was. It was simple: Score points. Why spend a lot of time doing so – thereby increasing the margin of error – when points could be accumulated quickly instead? Now, you might be thinking, "To score so many points, set so many records, and have his offensive philosophy copied by so many coaches, he must have a bunch of creative plays," right? The answer is, perhaps, the greatest deviation from other coaches: In 99% of collegiate and professional football teams, the coach or the offensive coordinator has a large, laminated play sheet with hundreds of plays in various formations and play types for every type of situation.

Leach has a napkin, or a small piece of paper.

He writes the couple of plays that he plans to use on that napkin. That's it.

The plays can run out of different formations, but Leach knows that his goal is to score points, so he writes down the plays that he believes will get to that result as fast as possible. If a play doesn't work, and he no longer believes it will serve the intended purpose, then he crosses it off the list. He isn't worried about the defense knowing the plays. He trusts his team to execute the play and get the result.

How can we simplify the process of improving our skillsets so we can get the touchdowns in our lives? How do you do what Mary Barra did and move more efficiently by reducing ten pages of rhetoric down to two words that help you carry out your task or improve upon your talent? How do you coach your future like Mike Leach and only equip yourself with the plays and tools you need to win in life instead of filling your brain with a lot of "possibilities" that don't move you toward your actual goal?

Conventional wisdom says that more is more, but success and opportunity understand that doing less helps accomplish more.

FIND

"Victory comes from finding opportunity in problems."
-Sun Tzu

CHAPTER 13
EVERY PROBLEM HAS A WEAKNESS

Diamonds are the hardest naturally occurring substance on Earth. The term "diamond" is derived from the Greek word "*adamas*", which roughly translates to "unconquerable or invincible". Having been marveled since the 4th century BC in India because of their beauty, diamonds were used as jewelry, as well as cutting tools because of their hardness. They were believed to possess mythical qualities to fight off evil and keep soldiers safe in battle.

Originally, diamonds were only believed to have originated in India, making them valuable to traders along the Silk Road, a land trading route that stretched from South East Asia, through East Africa into Southern Europe. In the 1700s, diamonds were discovered in Brazil, and in the late 1800s, a miner in Africa found a diamond.

As knowledge of diamonds becoming available in other parts of the world grew, investors and miners all over the globe started mining for diamonds. On January 26th, 1905, the superintendent of the Premier Mine in South Africa, captain Frederick Wells, saw what appeared to be a shard of glass sticking out of a mine only 9 meters from the surface. Using a pocketknife, he continued to scrape away until he had uncovered a 3,106.75-carat uncut diamond that weighed approximately 1.3 pounds.

The diamond, known as the Cullinan diamond in honor of Thomas Cullinan, the owner of the mine, quickly became famous. The diamond was eventually presented to King Edward VII and given to him as a gift to heal tensions between Britain and South Africa after the Boer War.

King Edward had the uncut diamond cut and polished, resulting in some of the most prestigious stones in existence today. The Cullinan 1, nicknamed the Great Star of Africa, is a 530.2 carat pear-shaped stone that still to this day sits atop the Sovereign's Sceptre with the Cross, the Sceptre used by British Kings and Queens in Royal coronation ceremonies. The value of the clear stone is believed to be around $400 million.

The Cullinan Diamond — one of the most valuable diamonds on the planet — is a marvel of exceptional color and clarity. To be so revered by British royalty — who boasts a collection named the "Crown Jewels", an extraordinary collection of 140 unique jewels with a value of billions of dollars — the diamond must truly stand out. If you look at the $400M diamond in it's all its glory as it sits in an exhibit in the Tower of London, you may assume that it's a perfect diamond.

Here's the secret. It's not. Though on the outside it looks completely clear in color, or D, a grade given by diamond graders to denote the diamond as "potentially flawless" with it's clear color, careful examination of the diamond found a number of imperfections including several small cleavages, known as glitzes, and some colorless graining on the surface as well.

Think about that for a second. Arguably the most epic and celebrated "perfect" diamond of all time, a diamond that was so hard that the tools used to cut it initially broke, the same diamond that is hand-selected and adorned by elite Royalty of Great Britain, has flaws too.

The diamond has flaws; we have flaws, and, more importantly, the adversities whom we try and overcome, the problems and trials that we face, and the giants whom we must conquer have flaws, too! Nothing is unconquerable. Everything and everyone has flaws. This isn't to shame you or to make you feel inferior; on the contrary, this is to help you understand one of the most defining pillars of finding opportunity.

Your problems, no matter how big or impossible they seem, have flaws too. If you can learn to find the flaws in your doubt, your problems, your adversities, you can find a competitive advantage – you can find a way to win.

ACHILLES' HEEL

In Greek Mythology, Achilles was one of the greatest warriors of all time. In the iconic novel, Iliad by Homer, Achilles is celebrated for his many victories in the Trojan War. Legend has it that when Achilles was a baby, his mother grabbed him by the heel and dipped him in the Styx river, a body of water in the underworld thought to have mystic powers. As a result, Achilles was almost invincible. No arrow or sword could pierce his body because of the magic protection he received from the river. No part that is, except for his Heel, the small area under his calf, above his foot where his mother had held him when she dunked him in the water as a baby.

Achilles killed many of Troy's greatest warriors throughout the Trojan War. Many began to think he couldn't be defeated. However, the Greek god Apollo, the most important of the gods, knew otherwise. He knew Achilles' weakness. While the rest of the soldiers feared his strength, Apollo focused on vulnerability. During a fateful battle, Paris of Troy, a Trojan prince, shot an arrow toward the legendary Achilles. Apollo guided the arrow as it struck Achilles right in the heel, the wound ultimately killing him.

The Achilles tendon, the tendon stretching from the heel to the back of the calf, got its name from Achilles. In modern days, The Achilles' heel is used to describe the weakness of an individual or business. It could be physical, emotional, spiritual, or a result of ethics.

Athletic teams often try and hide their Achilles' heel with well-devised game plans. Businesses hide their Achilles' heel with elaborate marketing plans designed to highlight the great features and benefits of their product or service in hopes of overshadowing glaring weaknesses. As individuals, we often try and hide our weaknesses from partners, from employers, from enemies and competitors.

The adversity you're facing that you feel is the end of the world, the lack of career advancement opportunity you claim to have because of that boss that hates you, and the genetics that you say to keep you from having the body you want, all have weaknesses. The problem is that, like the Trojan Warriors, we look at the proverbial warrior we're facing and think that it can't be beaten. But what would happen if modeled ourselves after Apollo and identified the weakness in our opponent and focused solely on attacking theirs?

Great salesman practice this often. They understand that the majority of customers have a preset list of excuses and objections that the customer hides behind like armor. Great salesman don't worry about those objections because the Achille's Heel of most buyers is rooted in a psychological concept coined by Sigmund Freud in 1895. Freud concluded through his research that people make decisions for two reasons. One, to gain pleasure. Two, to avoid pain.

The salesman understands that hiding behind those objections is a buyer that is at least interested in the product or service and needs the validation that it is the correct purchase for their needs and desires. Through qualifying questions and negotiations that target the potential customer's objections, the best salesman accurately identifies whether the potential customer is using the purchase to avoid pain or to gain pleasure. If the salesman is successful in their assessment of the customer, they often make the sale.

As a speaker and professional development leader at some of the largest Fortune 500 companies in the world, I can usually tell the state of a company I am going to speak to by the preliminary talks we have. When a company tries to deflect from their weaknesses, often called pain points in the corporate world, and ask me to lecture on other topics, I know the real weakness is in leadership. Great companies do the opposite. They are very aware of their pain points, and that's the exact reason they bring me in. As a result, we work together to alleviate or lessen that pain point so that they function more effectively, increase the bottom line, and, most importantly, fend them from competitors looking to seize on their weakness.

Pain points aren't just limited to buyers and large businesses. It's instinctual in all humans and animals in the world. On the plains of the Serengeti, animals understand there are a time and place for everything. Sometimes, a family of lions separates a wildebeest from the herd and attack with full confidence, leading to a pleasurable meal. However, if the herd of fleeing wildebeest change direction and stampede back toward the lion, instinct tells the lions to run or risk extreme pain or worse.

Lions, Fortune 500 companies, and experienced buyers all have weaknesses. What separates those lions from other animals and those great companies from failing companies, is knowing and understanding that they have weaknesses.

The ultimate weakness isn't in having pain points. The ultimate weakness is ignoring or denying that an Achilles' heel exists. But they do exist. Earlier in this book, we asked ourselves questions that made us question the limits we had set for ourselves and the lies we previously told ourselves. We uncovered some of these Achilles' heels in ourselves. Through understanding, shifting our mindsets, and sharpening our toolset, we continue to minimize the weaknesses.

But what about your opponent? What about that unsolvable problem at work, that impossible client, those unruly students, or that unconquerable obstacle? Yes, it may be a problem, a client, a student, or an obstacle. Still, if you will analyze and look for the weakness that it's guaranteed to have, you won't find it isn't unsolvable, impossible, unruly, or unconquerable. Don't fight the warrior, fight the warrior's weakness.

DON'T HOLD YOUR HEAD UP; HOLD YOUR BREATH

While I'd love it if we all had the time and patience to philosophize about the Achilles' heel of our problems while we sit in our study, smoking from a corncob pipe, as though we were Sherlock Holmes trying to solve a case, the reality is that most of us live fast. We juggle many responsibilities; we are often overextended; we have a lot on our plate, and we are forced to solve our problems and face our giants while on-the-go. How do we find the time to locate the Achilles' heel when we're fighting for our lives just to keep our heads above water?

I found the answer in the warm, Hawaiian waters of the Pacific Ocean.

Most likely, I'll never be asked to join the World Surf League and compete in international surfing competitions in huge waves, but I do enjoy surfing. One of the greatest lessons I learned when originally learning how to surf is one that has served me tremendously not only on a surfboard but also when finding opportunities in life.

After originally teaching me the basics of positioning on the surfboard and the mechanics behind standing up on a board, my teacher taught me the most important aspect of surfing and a fundamental cornerstone of opportunity locating. He said, "Baylor, WHEN you fall off the surfboard, don't try and get back to the surface as fast as you can, that's how you die." What?! I thought to myself. This guy is crazy, not only does he want me to NOT get back to the surface, he's telling me that if I do, I can die?!" That made no sense.

He explained to me that the reason many of the new surfers that drown, do so because they try and come to the surface too quickly. What they fail to realize is that waves come in sets, or groups, and often come in intervals of three to seven waves. When a surfer falls and immediately rises, he is hit by the remaining waves in the set, causing panic, swallowing water, and in the most tragic cases, death by drowning.

The reason waves come in groups comes from how waves are formed. Waves are primarily generated by the wind. Several factors such as wind speed, the distance the waves have traveled, and the period between waves (known as the wavelengths) affect how large the waves get. As it travels, a wave often swallows smaller, slower waves, so the waves become part of the larger' wave set. Waves cannibalize each other in deep water as they move toward the shore. The sets often come from the same direction or storm, thus giving them consistency in how they approach the beach in different seasons.

My instructor helped me understand that If I try and rebound too quickly, I'm being hit with one wave right after another, in a never-ending onslaught of waves that seek to create my downfall. You've no doubt probably felt that way in some aspects of your life. Financially, you're trying to get ahead but are hit with unsuspecting and relentless bills. You try and devote more time to work to advance in your career, but family and other obligations force you to divide your time. In each situation, you think the waves keep coming, and you have no time to get your head above water, much less find the Achilles' heel in the waves of life.

"What's the solution," I asked? He told me, "when you fall and go underwater, relax, and hold your breath." He explained to me the most important thing to do is to get your bearings, figure out which way is up, and let the waves pass, and then raise up to the surface between wave sets. The larger the waves, the longer you must hold your breath. Pro surfers, who surf enormous waves, condition themselves to hold their breath for several minutes.

When I took his advice, I found that it was peaceful under the waves. Though on the surface, they were crashing into the shore, underneath it was calm. He was right. When I let them pass, I came up in calm waters and was able to reset myself and attack the next waves.

You can apply the same principles to your life. The waves of life are constantly in motion. If you analyze your situation, you will realize that you aren't drowning in problems because of a relentless attack; it's because you try to rise up quickly and fight. Although it's admirable, it is the reason you're drowning. Finding opportunity isn't about how fast you can get up after you fall; it's about where and when you rise after you fall. There is calm between the waves of problems and the storms of the adversities that you face. If you give yourself time, you'll find the void between the waves, the Achilles' heel in the problems, and the flaw in your opponent's or competitor's strategy against you.

Remember, finding opportunity isn't always about keeping your head above water; sometimes, it's about how long you can hold your breath.

CHAPTER 14
WIN FROM ANYWHERE

A good friend of mine, Mark Carroll, is an avid student of Brazilian Jiu-Jitsu. Brazilian Jiu-Jitsu, or BJJ, is martial art with an emphasis on grappling and ground-fighting vs. using punches and kicks. The self-defense martial art uses leverage, technique, and holds to ensure that a smaller person can defend themselves against a larger opponent.

I always joked with Mark that I was going to come out one day and spar, or "roll" as it's called in BJJ. One day he called me out on it and invited me out to take a class. He said they'd even give me a Gi, the traditional outfit you picture when you think about The Karate Kid. I was ecstatic. I grew up playing Street Fighter, watching Jean Claude van Damme in all his martial arts movies, and reading Bruce Lee books, so I knew I was going to be an instant star. I even went as far as to look on Amazon for a black belt, (thankfully it didn't arrive in time.)

Admittedly, going into the session, I wasn't 100% sure what BJJ was. I assumed it was another martial art, just like the others. I couldn't have been more incorrect. Five minutes into the warmup, which consisted of me learning how to fall correctly and all sorts of other counter-intuitive moves, I was already gassed and out of breath. Why did I need to learn how to fall? Isn't the goal of learning some ninja skills to be able to dominate your opponent?

They taught me the reason you must learn how to fall correctly is that in life, you might not see the attack. We can all be blindsided and knocked down. In fact, in 87% of street fights or attacks, the fight goes to the ground. The reason you learn how to fall correctly is so that in case you are knocked down, you can displace the weight of the fall, prevent your head from hitting the ground and give yourself a chance to defend yourself.

Conventional wisdom in life teaches us that if you're knocked down, you're in the losing position. BJJ said we all get knocked down, what can you do from there? By learning how to fall, you learn that fighting from your back isn't a disadvantage at all, it's merely a different position to fight from. Feeling good about learning how to fall, I was ready for competition, or so I thought.

The class gathered around, and I was introduced to the instructor, João Pedro Rodrigues, known in the BJJ world as "Somalia" because of his lanky, skinny frame. Somalia, a black-belt (the highest level you can reach in BJJ), weighed over 100 lbs. less than my 6'4, 245 lb. frame, and I towered above him by almost a foot. Mark told me I could "roll" with him. In my mind, I thought, "here's my chance. If I can beat a 5-time world champion in my first lesson, I'll become an instant legend." We squared off. I knew I had the reach on him due to my superior height and length. He stood there patiently as I closed in. Finally,

I reached in to grab him thinking he'd try and dodge me. Instead, he fell back as I moved forward, grabbed me, and the next thing I know, I'm being flipped into the air as he rolled back and sent me to the other side of the mat.

I thought, "*WHAT JUST HAPPENED?!*" I got up, determined to try again, but something was different. Somalia didn't get up all. He lay there calmly on the mat with his hands and legs up, encouraging me to try to get him. I was confused. Why would someone half my size *want* me to try to get him while he lay on the ground? Wasn't being on the ground bad? The problem is, I couldn't get him. He used his legs to keep me away. For the next few minutes, I tried everything in my power to either grab him, smother him, or do anything I could think of to win.

No matter the position he was in, he found a way to twist me, flip me, or make some superhuman move to change the dynamic and put himself in control, regardless of how we started.

Over the course of the class, I learned a valuable lesson that applies to all of us in any situation. Society says that to win, you must be the biggest, strongest, fastest, most funded, or any other "advantageous" quality. Plainly put, to win, you must be on top. What I learned in BJJ was quite the opposite. Not once in training did the students ever start while both standing and facing each other. They never started "equal." In every learning situation, one student either started on his back or started on a knee with the other student behind them. Normally we would think to have someone behind you or over you meant trouble, and normally we'd be correct. But BJJ teaches people to not only fight from those positions but to win.

If you're skilled and know what an opportunity looks like, you can win from anywhere.

Imagine looking at your current predicament or perceived disadvantages and picturing it as the most advantageous situation you could be in? While on your back In BJJ, you have an advantage because your legs are longer and stronger than your opponents' arms. If an opponent is on top of you, contrary to the normal response of trying to push them off you, BJJ artists pull the opponent on top of them and keep them tight. The reasoning behind this is that if the opponent can't separate themselves from you, they can't get momentum to strike or hurt you. Essentially, you take away the advantage the opponent on top of you has.

It doesn't stop there. Great students and BJJ fighters are constantly watching your arms and legs. Not just to avoid your advance, they are looking for an opportunity… the one small mistake you make. Leave a leg or arm exposed, and next thing you know, you're in an armbar trying to submit. Distance yourself a bit but not enough, and next thing you know, you have legs and an arm wrapped around your neck, choking you out.

In any situation, from any position, skilled BJJ fighters can win. They can because they realize that size, height, position, and all the other perceived-advantageous factors don't matter. They are irrelevant because the fighters know what an opportunity looks like. They train to spot the one mistake the opponent makes, and the entire situation changes instantly.

You may feel you're in the fight of your life. Are you hopelessly swinging and punching and hoping for the best? Are you constantly trying to "get on top," assuming that's the only way to win? Rather than wasting energy trying to get on top, ask yourself, how can I win from this position? What does the opportunity look like that I could capitalize on when it comes?

Here are some of the important keys to remember if you're looking to win regardless of how you start or how far behind you think you are.

1. **PERSPECTIVE IS DECEIVING.** Often in life, we think that having our back against the wall or not having the right resources or teams are valid reasons to be at a disadvantage. But what if we learned that no matter the position we're in, we have an opportunity and advantage? Train your mind to start searching for the opportunity. Are you a small business owner, competing against corporate giants? Good! You're small; you can move and pivot quickly when the market changes. A speedboat can always turn faster than a cruise ship. Are you an entrepreneur who's underfunded, compared to your competitors? Good! You've learned the value of a dollar and how to be more frugal with money, and you can put more thought into how your money is spent. Don't have as much experience as the people in your office whom you're competing with for a raise or promotion? Good! You can let your superiors know that you aren't stuck in your ways and can learn and adapt the company methodology quicker because you don't have to break old habits and methods of operation first. No matter how bad you think life is, there's always an advantage to being in your position.

2. **IT'S NOT THE SIZE OF THE DOG IN THE FIGHT; IT'S THE EXPERIENCE OF THE FIGHT IN THE DOG.** In my sparring session with the 5-time Brazilian Jiu-Jitsu world champion, he smiled as we began to roll because he knew something I didn't. Was I stronger? Yes. Was I bigger and more intimidating looking? Absolutely. Did it matter? No, because he knew what he was doing. Experience beats genetics. Training beats strength. Knowledge beats brute force. You may not be the richest, smartest, or most connected person in life, but you can always become a master of your craft and defeat the competition in any facet of life.

3. **LIFE CAN CHANGE QUICKLY.** I saw it time and time again. As I watched the students grapple with each other, several times, a student who was in a perceived winning position, made one small, costly error and the momentum and victory shifted to the opponent. Never count yourself out just because you're down. Life is about information and execution.

4. **WHEN LIFE GETS HECTIC, YOU DON'T RISE TO THE OCCASION;** you fall to the level of your training. Study hard, train hard, practice hard. When you become a master of your craft, you learn how to spot the opportunity, and more importantly, you know when to strike on that opportunity.

5. **FIND WHAT WORKS FOR YOU.** Joao Pedro is not a big guy. If I had to guess, I'd say he's maybe 5'5, 135 lbs. He's no Lebron James. On paper, it would appear that there's no way he'd ever be able to become a professional athlete due to his size. But that didn't stop him from finding an opportunity for himself. He ignored societal

norms and found what worked for him. If you watched the 2016 Summer Olympics in Rio De Janeiro, Brazil, then you undoubtedly heard about the "Favelas," which were the equivalent of the worst hoods in America. Joao grew up just a step above those, and he said that he could count on one hand the number of friends he'd grown up with who were still alive. Rather than participate in the violence, gang activity, or drugs that his friends did, he rode his bicycle seven miles to the BJJ gym every day. Disciplined training and commitment afforded him access to fights outside of Brazil. He turned that access into opportunity and began winning world championships. He then parlayed that opportunity into a career as an elite pro fighter. In the same way, you can utilize your strengths in life and turn them into access to a better life, an opportunity for a better future, and ultimately, a career doing what you love. Joao does it, and you can, too. We may never be world championship fighters with black belts, but we can bring the same discipline to our craft and create opportunities from it. However, to do this, we must truly commit. We must live it; we must breathe it; it must be in our DNA. As Joao told me in his cool, thick, Brazilian accent, *"You have to be an example to someone. Everything you say; you need to be first."*

There is an opportunity to win in every situation *if* you continue to study your craft and learn what that opportunity looks like. Dispel the myth that you must constantly be fighting to get to the top and instead relax and seek to use leverage – not force – as the opportunity presents itself. A guy half my size flipped me into the air. In the same manner, you can flip the competition or industry on its head if you focus on improving your skillset, learning what the opportunity looks like, and capitalizing on the mistakes of your competitors and your industry the split-second in which you see an opening.

CHAPTER 15
SHARK THEORY

I host a twice-weekly mindset development podcast called "Shark Theory". I don't know if it's because of the perception of sharks from the movie *Jaws*, or the TV show "Shark Tank", or a combination of the two, but most people think the podcast is about being a fierce, relentless predator in pursuit of your goals. People are often shocked to find out the reason for the name "Shark Theory" is based on the movement and mindset of real sharks, which is contrary to their preconceived notions.

We all have that person or people in our lives that we identify as "sharks." It could be the go-getter in the office, the hustler friend that's always working, or that driven friend who will stop at nothing to reach their goals. I applaud the effort, but the label of the shark couldn't be further from the truth.

I'm obsessed with sharks. Shark Week on the Discovery channel is the one series that has me glued to the TV each year. They are big, scary, menacing, always on the go, eating and destroying everything in their path.

Or are they? Over the last few years, I've studied sharks, specifically Great Whites, and found the notions we have about them are incorrect. First, we believe that sharks sprint through the water always in search of whatever is in front of them. The reality, however, is that sharks aren't ever in a hurry. Not only that, but sharks don't eat anything and everything in their path, on the contrary, they hunt specific prey. Too often we spin our wheels, sprinting after every "opportunity" and chasing everything that crosses our path, for fear of missing out. As a result, we often pursue good opportunities and miss out on great ones.

What would happen if you took a shark approach to your goals? What if you were patiently progressive, moving forward always but not concerning yourself with every opportunity, but only focusing on those that you truly want? Wouldn't you save time? Wouldn't the result be so much better in having achieved goals that you wanted instead of crossing off checklist items for the sake of saying you completed a task? Do you see the difference?

Realizing the misconceptions that we had about sharks and wanting to know more, I decided that I needed to see the sharks for myself. I visited award-winning charter captain, Michael "Sharky" Marquez, of Out Cast Charters in the Gulf of Mexico, to go shark fishing. I had no desire to keep a shark; I just wanted to learn about them and experience them firsthand, so I could apply the principles of their behavior to my pursuit of improvement and opportunity.

Keep in mind that I've never fished a day in my life, nor had my brother, who joined us on this fishing expedition. The lessons I learned taught were some of the best experiences of finding an opportunity that I ever had. We began by fishing for redfish and other fish that we could eat so that: (a) we could learn how to use a fishing pole; and (b) we'd have dinner.

Side note: Though we would ultimately catch redfish to eat, we lost some of them when pelicans stole the fish while I taped a podcast episode live on the pier with Captain Sharky. I can't blame the pelicans; they're opportunists, too! Haha!

A few hours into the charter, Michael told us, "Okay, it's time to catch sharks." He then replaced our fishing poles with some larger, thicker fishing poles with stronger lines, and we headed out into deeper water.

KNOW WHERE TO LOOK

My brother and I stared blankly at each other, partly excited, partly nervous because of how big these fishing poles were. It's one thing to say you want to catch a shark; it's a different story when the opportunity comes along. Isn't that true of opportunity? How many times do we say we want one, but when it comes time to act, we freeze up? If that's you, understand it happens to us all. The best way to overcome that fear or that hesitation is to continue to put yourself in the direct path of opportunity. With experience comes peace of mind and an ability to act quickly.

I had my reservations. I don't know how many sharks I thought there were in the world, but I thought, "How in the world in this vast ocean will we find a shark just swimming around who happens to take our bait?" But Captain Sharky wasn't worried at all. Why? He knew where to look. He said that in the area where we were, sharks hung out in two places: (1) a lot of sharks followed shrimp boats, which dragged the ocean floor and created easy meals for the sharks; and (2) they hung out in an old military ocean-dumping ground.

On that day, there were no shrimp boats, so we headed toward the military dumping ground. I was looking for floating sea buoys that said "caution, military dump" or something to that effect to let us know we had arrived in the correct spot, but I saw nothing. At a certain point, Michael killed the engines and announced, we're here. Huh? How did he know? There were no distinguishing marks, and we were far out in the water. But that taught me a valuable lesson. The more you do something, the more experience you gain, the more you'll instinctually become aware of where opportunity is. Captain Sharky didn't need an instrument or a guide to find the area, the fact that he had been there hundreds if not thousands of times was all he needed. As a result of experience, he KNEW where to look. In your life, repetition will help you begin to identify areas of opportunity, as well.

USE THE RIGHT BAIT

You don't catch sharks with worms or minnows, like regular fish. But what do sharks eat? I had never really thought about it before; I assumed that they ate whatever they felt like eating. But again, Michael's experience taught me another lesson. He knew in advance that we wanted to catch sharks, so for the few days before, he had been stockpiling the type of bait that the sharks in the area responded to: Stingrays and some other types of fish that he knew the sharks would be hungry for were applied to the ends of the fishing rods.

In the areas of opportunity that you're seeking in life, are you using the right bait? Are you doing your part to make yourself, your product, or your service desirable to the marketplace? Too often, we make the mistake of putting out the bait — the advertisements or proclamations that would appeal to us — but we don't consider what is attractive to the opportunity we are looking for. Isn't it better to attract opportunity than to chase it?

Through studying, observation, and learning from others ahead of you, you can analyze the patterns of the opportunity you're after to figure out which bait is best to attract it. In business, analysts study consumer behavior in detail. Digital advertisers monitor web traffic, purchase history, and social media topic interaction to gain an in-depth understanding of how you think and feel, and what triggers you to buy. Why? So that they can serve you relevant ads to make you spend more money.

Have you ever visited a website and almost made a purchase and then at the last minute decided against it? Maybe it was too expensive, perhaps you didn't want to make an impulsive purchase, maybe you wanted to shop around a bit more, but what happens? All of a sudden, every ad on social media is about that product. Your email is about that product. Everywhere you look, the product is in your face, with reinforced benefits and features and a simple checkout process. Eventually, you cave in, after all, on second thought, you do need that item or service right, now don't you?

What changed? Advertisers, especially in the digital age, use your mind against you. Is this some new age philosophy? No, they use cognitive dissonance against you. The Cognitive Dissonance Theory, discovered by Leon Festinger in 1957, demonstrates that the human mind yearns for consistency in your beliefs, opinions, and general attitude. When your attitudes and beliefs differ, your brain takes action to get them in alignment. Think about the last time, "your heart," and "your head" conflicted. It kept you up at night, didn't it? We agonize in situations where we know one thing to be correct, but deep down, we wish for the opposite to be true.

In the Cognitive Dissonance Theory, we learn that the mind, when faced with two opposing beliefs, will lean toward siding with the idea that brings the most pleasure, aka the "lesser of two evils." A common example used to illustrate the theory is a person who smokes cigarettes. The person knows for a fact that cigarettes are harmful to their health and can lead to various forms of cancer and other illnesses. Still, they continue to smoke, why? Because, on the flip side, is the calmness or elated feeling they instantly receive from the nicotine. The mind must decide, long term health issues, or instant happiness?

The decision comes down to reinforcement, which is often a product of what helps us today. Our mind is wired to seek immediate pleasure over that of the long term. YOLO, or "you only live once," is a phrase our mindset tells us to justify the decision to light up another cigarette.

Those digital marketers use a blanket of ads to reinforce to you the desire to purchase that product. Ultimately, with enough reinforcement, aka more ads, your mind says, "pleasure comes with this product, I can always make more money later," and you click BUY. You have your new product, and your mind is happy because it no longer must choose between two dissenting options, it is now back in perfect harmony.

Whether you're a salesman looking to attract customers, a business looking to build clientele, or a fisherman looking for the monster catch of a lifetime, using the correct bait is a significant step to locate opportunity.

LEARN HOW TO FIGHT

Michael told us that the sharks would be there shortly. Here's what you need to know: Sharks don't attack linearly, like most fish; they come from underneath. Unlike most fish that grab the bait and consider the fight to be over, sharks gain extreme velocity, take the bait, and swim off with alarming speed.

How fascinating is that? Most of us are happy just reaching our goal, while sharks explode through their target. Back in college, our football strength and conditioning coach at Baylor University would always reinforce to us during our sprints at the end to run "through the line, not to the line." What he was saying is the job isn't over just because you reached the destination, you must finish past your goal. Don't let up and come to a stop at your goal; hit your objective at full force.

As a result of how sharks attack the bait, Michael said that we must let them take the bait for a period before we try to yank the fishing rod and reel them in. Once reeled in, our captain explained that it was going to be a tough fight; we couldn't just reel in the shark as hard and fast as we could because the shark was going to fight for freedom. If we pulled, and it was pulling the opposite way, then the line will snap, and we'd lose the shark. To catch it, we must let the shark swim away until it got tired. Once it was tired, we could reel it in. When the shark got a second wind, we'd allow it to swim. We'd repeat the process over and over, until we got the shark close to the boat.

If you're like me, you have a "reel it in as fast as I can" mentality when it comes to success. We get close to a sale, close to our goal, close to an opportunity, and we abandon the strategy. The opportunity took the bait, and we don't know how to fight to the finish. Lasting success is a patient fight; it's not a brute-force reel. Great boxers stay patient and look for their opponent to drop their guard before striking. Great investors study markets and trends before making long term investment decisions. Everyone who succeeds on a long-term scale plays the patient game. They learn how to fight; they don't deviate from their strategy just because "they get a bite."

Understand that getting initial interest or getting your first hint of opportunity doesn't mean you've captured it. Though hooking a fish to the line is the first step, though getting that initial buzz or client interaction is a milestone, you must compose yourself and have an action plan to close the deal or reel in the shark.

Do you have a defined process? Learn from those around you if not. Luckily, Captain Sharky was an expert angler and taught me the process or I wouldn't have ever caught a shark. No matter your industry, genre, or goal, there is someone out there or some material out there to teach you the process of the fight to ensure success when the opportunity arises.

IT'S NOT OVER UNTIL THE SHARK IS IN THE BOAT

I remember the first time I closed a major deal for a speaking engagement with a Fortune 500 company. We agreed on the terms; we decided on the date, and I celebrated as though I'd won an NBA Championship. I took friends out that night to celebrate my achievement; I shopped as though I'd already gotten the check, and I went to bed with a smile on my face.

But then, something happened. Days and weeks went by, and communication with the company was minimal. As it turned out, the person who had agreed to book me left the company. The person sent to replace her wanted to go in a different direction with their professional development. My services were no longer needed. Not only that; I didn't have a contract in place. I was out of luck.

That tragedy taught me that it's never over until it's over. In business, it's not over until the check has cleared, and the service has been performed. In health, it's not over until the goal weight is reached, and a new, healthy lifestyle becomes a way of life.

"It isn't over until the shark is in the boat," the captain told us. What he was saying is that 90% of the sharks that get free from the line do so within the last few feet of the boat. The sharks are exhausted; they have been reeled in, and just when you think it's over, they summon their final energy and make one last push for freedom.

How many times have you quit when it seemed hopeless? How many times — when on the brink of financial disaster, relationship failure, or giving up on a goal — did you throw in the towel? "Throwing in the towel" is a concept used in boxing. When a trainer sees that there is no chance at victory for the fighter he trains, he throws a towel into the ring to signal to the referee to stop the fight to prevent further damage to his fighter.

You must develop a mindset of not even bringing a towel to the battle — meaning under no circumstance will you give up. Sharks have that mindset. As a result, so many "surefire catches" result in sharks breaking free.

Think about those times you gave up on the goals you wanted because they looked impossible. What if you would have given one more herculean effort? What if that one extra push, the one additional phone call, that one extra email, that one extra mile on the treadmill sparked the freedom you were looking for and helped you reach the goal?

Study the habits of opportunity, so you'll know where to look. Arm yourself with the correct bait to lure in opportunities. Understand and execute the process of fighting to capitalize on those opportunities and stay patient in the fight until the shark is in the boat, the money's in the bank, or the goal is crossed off your bucket list.

CREATE

"Don't wait for the right opportunity. Create it."
-George Bernard Shaw

CHAPTER 16
BECOME AN ENEMY
OF THE NORM

Standing at 6'2, 218 lbs., Trevor Berbick was a force to be reckoned with. With an already illustrious career that included a trip to the Olympics as a boxer for Jamaica and scoring a victory over the great Muhammad Ali in Ali's final fight, Trevor was an emerging star. Although he was an underdog, on March 22, 1986, he shocked the world by easily defeating the current WBC World Heavyweight Champion, Pinklon Thomas, to become the new heavyweight boxing champion of the world.

On November 22nd of the same year, he made his first title defense, and the world was watching. Trevor had a three-inch height advantage and a seven-inch reach advantage. Having arms that were 7 inches longer than his opponent would give Trevor the opportunity to keep his distance from his opponent and still be able to throw punches without being hit in return. His opponent was a young twenty-year-old, lacking the experience of the 32-year old Trevor. Berbick had a simple strategy for defeating his opponent. He would use his size advantage to push his opponent backward and use his length advantage to pummel his opponent. If his opponent got close to him, he'd lean on the challenger and further exhaust him. When the challenger was frustrated and tired, Trevor he would go in strong to finish him off.

It was a solid game plan, and on paper, it seemed like it would be effective. However, this was no ordinary challenger. Standing across the ring, 16 feet away stood a menacing opponent wearing black shorts, black shoes, no socks, and fire in his eyes. His challenger, Iron Mike Tyson, had a different plan. Seek and Destroy.

The nose, primarily responsible for the respiratory system in the body, is not designed to withstand punches. The symptoms of being punched in the nose are far greater than just a swollen nose or restricted breathing. When a person is punched in the nose with great force, their vision suffers. Because of the nose's placement, immediate headaches can occur instantly, and numbness and loss of function of the arms are possible too.

Mike Tyson knew this. He wasn't worried about the larger opponent or the perceived disadvantages he had in reach according to what boxing calls "the tale of the tape," which is the measurements of each boxer, height, weight, and a reach to show who should have the advantage. Iron Mike knew that if he aimed for that 2-inch nose, the strategy and advantages of the champion wouldn't matter. That's exactly what he did.

The starting bell rang, and Mike Tyson immediately started throwing heavy punches right to the nose of Trevor Berbick. A few seconds into the fight, all the advantages and all the strategy went away. Trevor was in a fight for his life. Winning wasn't an option; he was trying to *survive*.

Very quickly in the second round, Tyson knocked out Trevor and became the youngest heavyweight champion in boxing history. Tyson said it best: *"Everybody has a plan until they get punched in the nose."*

BREAKING THE STATUS QUO

The status quo – Latin for "the existing state of affairs" – affects us in every aspect of our lives. In our professional careers, we often go with the flow of what our bosses, company, or industry does. In our personal lives, we become creatures of habit and are set in our ways when it comes to our interactions with family, friends, and neighbors. We set status quos for ourselves with our health, diet, exercise (or lack thereof), and schedule. How often have you made an excuse, such as, "I just don't have enough time," or "That's just how I am"?

But is it, though? Are the choices you make that prevent you from reaching your peak state or chasing your potential truly a character flaw? To accept that it's "how you are" means would mean you're incapable of change. But is that the truth?

The reality is we become comfortable in our lives, for better or worse, because even if we're unhappy, we know what to expect. Have you ever hated your job? We no doubt all know someone who does nothing but complain about their job, their boss, and their coworkers. You probably think to yourself, "why don't they get another job?" The answer is perhaps the same reason you don't make changes you need to make or the reason you remain comfortable in the status quo – fear.

As we discussed in an earlier chapter, deep inside your brain, an almond-shaped group of neurons called the amygdala, is largely responsible for processing your emotions. Avoiding Pain? It starts with the amygdala. Are you chasing pleasure? You guessed it. It formulates in the amygdala as well. This area of the brain is responsible for your immediate reaction to a situation. When you hear a loud sound and immediately jump, the amygdala was at the heart of the fear emotion.

Think about the last time someone snuck up behind you and scared you. You undoubtedly jumped up immediately and turned around. What did your body do once you realized it was someone whom you knew and trusted? It relaxed. The reason is that after the amygdala processes an emotion, it passes the information along to a higher cortex in the brain, which makes decisions. This part of your brain combines the new information and stimuli from the amygdala and combines it with what it already knows, which is, "*I know this person; this person is safe.*" This tells the body, "*It's okay; we've seen this before; we are safe; let's relax.*" Simply put, when you experience something over and over, the fear decreases.

But what happens if someone snuck up behind us and when we turned around it was someone we didn't know or recognize? The amygdala would fire, send information to the higher cortical center of the brain, which would then issue an alert to the whole body "we don't know this situation, PANIC, RUN!"

So, what am I saying?

In our lives, we follow the status quo because though at one point it may have been scary to us, or disrespectful such as a condescending boss speaking horribly to us, eventually, the brain becomes used to it and accepts it as the norm. Since we're conditioned to avoid pain, and thus avoid the fear of anything that can bring pain, we settle for the norm.

But is that really what you want? Do you want to live a life predicated on accepting the rules and standards that society has set? Do you want to coast through life mindlessly? You wouldn't be reading this book if that's what you wanted. But how do we change it? How do we attack an industry that's bigger and stronger than us? How do we defeat our mental monsters that keep us depressed, fearful, or in a constant state of worry? How do we shock our system so that we can escape the monotony of our day-to-day routine and create new opportunities in our lives and careers?

PATTERN INTERRUPTION

We often fear change or fear to try to create opportunity, whether that be starting a new business, asking someone out on a date, moving to a new city, or starting a new exercise and diet program because we feel the odds are against us. Our competitors are too strong; the exercises are too hard; we're inferior to the person we want to pursue compared to others.

And maybe that's true. But what did Tyson do to defeat a larger opponent? He understood that size didn't matter if he aimed for the nose. We discussed earlier that everyone and every problem has an Achilles' heel, a point of attack that if you focus on, you can win. We've discussed that, like great Brazilian Jiu-jitsu fighters, you can win from any position. But how? How do we disrupt our industries so that we can create new opportunities for ourselves? How do we disrupt our own negative ways of thinking so that we can create new opportunities?

In neuro-linguistic programming (NLP), a science based on learning the language of the mind, it's called "pattern disruption." If we can learn the principles of breaking patterns, status quos, and norms, then we will create new opportunities for ourselves that might not have existed before. The late actor Heath Ledger, who played the famous Batman supervillain, Joker, in the Academy Award-winning movie, The Dark Knight, said it best: "*Introduce a little anarchy, upset the established order, and everything becomes chaos. I'm an agent of chaos, and you know why I love chaos? It's fair.*"

Now I'm not saying to go physically assault your competitors or engage in any illegal or immoral means of disrupting your industry, but you can follow this disruption blueprint to shake things and essentially deliver a Mike Tyson knockout punch to your status quo to create opportunity and become a champion in your life.

STUDY THE NORM

What is the current status quo? How does your industry or company operate? Are you making changes to yourself? What are your patterns and habits? Tyson knew what Trevor Berbick was going to try to do. He knew what all his opponents were going to try to do. The reason is he studied. Not only did he study his opponents, but he also studied all the greats in the history of the sport. Tyson was known to have a large film collection, and he studied in detail the nuances of all the great fighters. He learned tendencies of different types of fighters, and, as a result, he found weaknesses. He saw opportunities. You must have the same level of research as a prize fighter, looking for a small weakness or hesitations in an opponent's game plan; the same level of detail as scientists studying cells at a microscopic level, looking to find weaknesses in viral and bacterial strains so that vaccines, medicines, and cures can be found. You must study your industry with the same level of passion and devotion as a hedge fund analyst about to invest billions of dollars on behalf of their clients.

Sun Tzu said it best in his book, *The Art of War*: "*Know your enemy and know yourself, and you need not fear the result in a hundred battles*." Study the current standard to find weaknesses and areas of opportunity.

DETERMINE WHERE IT STARTS

In business, who's leading your industry? Who sets the trends and norms? In your personal life, what is the trigger to start your pattern? Think about it, long and hard. What is the moment that your day-to-day patterns begin? Is the moment that you sit down at your desk and log in to your computer at your job that you shut off your mind and join the rat race? Is it the second your alarm goes off that you pick up your phone and waste 30 minutes scrolling through social media sites? Is it the fact you knowingly visit the breakroom at the office mid-morning because you know Karen always brings cookies and treats, and you knowingly derail your diet as a result?

Determining the starting point is imperative because if you can locate the source of "the norm," you now have an attack point. Just like Tyson knew that if he focused on hitting Berbick in the nose, the size difference and all the other advantages that Trevor supposedly had, didn't matter. By finding the origination point of a status quo or bad habit, you're now able to focus all your energy on that. By doing so, you "create chaos" and give yourself a chance to win by minimizing the advantages of your competitors or your self-deprecating self-talk has over you. It's now you vs. a Nose, not you versus a competitor.

ATTACK HOW THEY LEAST EXPECT IT

The Greeks tried relentlessly to enter the city of Troy to defeat the Trojans. The walls were too high; the enemy was too strong; there was no way to attack the city from the outside. All who tried failed. This was the norm. For ten years, the Greeks tried to storm Troy, and for a decade, they failed. But then Epeius, a master carpenter, had a realization. The norm was to attack Troy from the outside, which is where Troy was the strongest. But no one had ever attacked them from the inside, where they had no defense.

He built a giant wooden horse, and inside of it, hid the greatest of the Greek warriors. The rest of the Greek soldiers retreated, pretending to have given up. The giant structure was given to Troy as a gift to Athena, the goddess of War. Trojan soldiers wheeled the giant Trojan horse into their own city gates. At night, when everyone slept, the Greek warriors escaped out of the Trojan horse opened the city gates from inside, and the Greek Soldiers rushed the city and became victorious.

The most lethal computer virus, a Trojan horse, works in quite the same manner. Rather than build a sophisticated virus that has to battle all of the anti-virus protection and layers of defense on top of a computer operating system, a Trojan horse sneaks in underneath the defenses and takes over the main functions of the operating system, giving the hacker complete control over the system.

What is your Trojan horse? How can you look at your habits, competition, and current hang-ups and attack them in a way you haven't before? Remember, every problem has a weakness, and usually, those problems or competitors seem strong because you've attacked them at their strengths, just like Greece attacked Troy at its strongest. But what if you could attack from an area where it's not prepared? Disruption results when you find that origin point and attack it in a different direction.

STAY RELENTLESS

Mike Tyson beat Trevor severely. He was relentless. He threw combination after combination. Berbick never knew what hit him, never got a chance to take a step back and remember his strategy or game plan. Tyson caused chaos. You can cause chaos by attacking your industry in a new way, fighting your previous self-defeating habits, and never letting up. Remember, the job isn't over until you've won.

When all things are equal, the best man wins. You're the best. Create chaos. Go for the knockout. Become the champion.

CHAPTER 17
BECOME A MONSTER

We're taught to fear monsters. In the 1933 movie (and countless remakes since), *King Kong*, the titular character is a 104-foot-tall gorilla that sends humans running away, screaming in utter fear. Godzilla, the prehistoric reptile, towers above Japan and incinerates everything in his path with his fiery breath. Frankenstein's monster terrorizes villages and strikes fear in the eyes all of those who see him. The Incredible Hulk smashes everything in his path. Every monster has some superhuman quality, whether it's size, strength, power, or some other advantage that they have over most people. The monsters understand that advantage; they combine it with the fear their opponents have of them and become larger than life.

To these monsters, fear is an ally.

Now chances are we'll never be forced to run from a 10-story gorilla or be forced to fight a neon green, superhuman strength Hulk, but monsters, whether real or imagined do exist. Perhaps the monster in your life is the boss, the industry-leading company in your genre, or your direct competition at your job, which is competing for the same raise, promotion, or customers as you. In my last book, Wintality, I devoted a chapter toward "mental monsters," the self-talk and nuances in our brain that often work against us. We fear monsters, partly because they have a strength or competitive advantage that we don't, and partially for another reason – we don't understand them.

But what if, instead of fearing the monsters, we became the monster? No, I'm not saying that you should decimate a city, physically destroy people around you, or invoke a villainous mindset, but what if you became keenly aware of your strengths, learned how to snap into a mindset that fueled those strengths, and used those "super-strengths" — combined with your competition's fear of them — to your advantage?

ORIGINS OF A DEEPER POWER

Moments before the ensuing battle, the crowd of almost 60,000 falls silent. There in the center of the pitch at Eden Park in Auckland, New Zealand, stands the All-Blacks, the national rugby team of New Zealand. Dressed in all black jerseys, black shorts, and black shoes, the All-Blacks stand in formation near center-pitch, facing their opponent.

The captain emerges towards the front of the team, each with their stares piercing into the eyes and souls of their opponents, and begins shouting orders in Maori, the language of the indigenous people of New Zealand.

Ringa pakia (the team slaps their thighs in unison)
Uma tiraha (the team puffs out their chest)
Turi whatia (everyone bends their knees)
Hope whai ake (everyone bends their hips)
Waewae takahia kia kino (the entire team Stomps their feet in unison)

And then it begins… Ka Mate, an ancient war cry of the Maori people.

Ka mate! Ka mate!
Ka ora! Ka ora!
Ka mate! Ka mate!
Ka ora! Ka ora!
Tenei Te Tangata Puhuru huru
Nana nei tiki mai
Whakawhiti te ra
A upa ne ka up ane
Upane, Kaupane
Whiti te ra

The battle cry translates to:

It is death! It is death!
It is life! It is life!
It is death! It is death!
It is life! It is life!
This is the hairy man who summons the sun and makes it shine
A step upward, another step upward!
A step upward, another... the Sun shines!

The All-Blacks are one of the most successful teams in the history of any professional sport. They have a winning percentage of 86 percent in the professional era. To the All Blacks, the haka is more than an intimidation tactic. It creates a state change in the team. If you watch the eyes of the team members, you see eyes bulging, tongues lashing, almost as if the warriors have become possessed by a greater power.

The reason for the state change is because the haka represents so much more. The haka, a ritualized dance often performed by the ancient Maori warriors before a battle, carried a theme that became a source of remembrance, power, and was believed to invoke the God of War to aid the warriors. Inia Maxwell, Maori Cultural Expert, and Ohinemutu Tribe leader say that each haka tells a unique story.

A popular haka that he teaches reminds the Warriors that they don't own the land, they are just passing through. But while they are here, they are the guardians of the land. The warriors carry the knowledge of their ancestors and fight to protect the legacy for future generations. They are of the land, and the land is of them.

The ritualistic dance gives the warriors preparing for battle, or the team preparing for a match, a sense of "it's bigger than me." By fighting to protect the honor of the past and fighting for the continued legacy of the future, the haka summons power behind the men in battle or athletes on the field.

Now, think for a second about which would be more powerful. Would you rather fight against someone who was competing solely for the sake of winning, or someone who was not only fighting for their legacy and lineages but fighting for the belief that the entire history of their culture was in their veins, fighting with them?

Whether it be from war, athletic competition, business, or any other adversity in life, we all get tired. In those times of extreme fatigue, if we are in it for ourselves, there's a chance that we will quit. But when we draw upon something deeper — the smiles and wellbeing of our loved ones, the hope for a better tomorrow, or the legacy we are leaving for those who will follow us — we gain an advantage. We harness the power of something deeper than ourselves.

In his book, "Legacy: What the All-Blacks can teach us about the business of life," Author James Kerr spent five weeks with the All-Blacks as they prepared for the Rugby World Cup, had this to say. "The haka reminds us of the inherent fragility of all life. How little time is given to each of us and how we still have so much to do. This is our time."

The All-Blacks understand the value of "now" and harness a deeper power to transform into a mindset that has created not only a legacy on the field of competition but a legacy and tradition that is admired and adored by an entire nation.

When you harness a power deeper than yourself, you unlock a superhuman aspect of yourself that can seize opportunity and create results that you want. Afterall, monsters don't apologize or ask for what they want. They make it happen.

SEE THE BEAUTY IN THE BEAST

The 1991 Classic Walt Disney Film, Beauty and the Beast, based on a French romantic fairy tale of the same name, tells the story of a prince who is transformed into a hideous beast as a result of his arrogance and is forced to go on a quest to find true love to unbreak the beastly spell. His love interest, Belle, who is originally held prisoner at his castle, sees deeper than the outward appearance and develops a relationship with the turned prince. After the two become close, the Beast allows her to leave the castle to aid her ailing father, thus believing she would never return.

In the epic final battle scene as the neighboring villagers, led by the pompous villain Gaston who is after the love of Belle as well, storm the castle to kill the Beast. The Beast, who is heartbroken at the thought of losing Belle, sees her return and regains his strength and wins the battle against the evil townspeople and is reunited with Belle, and the two live happily ever after.

That's a fairy tale; they always end that way, right? Yes, the story is a fictitious tale, but in it lies the first step in becoming the monster that's going to create the opportunities you want in life.

LOVE SOMETHING GREATER THAN YOURSELF

The Beast loved Belle and found strength in her. The All-Blacks possess a profound love of country, heritage, and the future that transforms them into some of the most all-time winning professional athletes in the world. You hear of parents gaining superhuman strength to save their children. Although the latter seems more myth than fact, there is science behind the truth of that ability. In the article "Stealth Superpowers", science writer Jeff Wise discovered that Tom Boyle, Jr. is proof of this superhuman feat.

After witnessing a 3,000 lb. Chevrolet Camaro hit a child, Tom saw the child's bicycle trapped under the vehicle. He sprinted over to the car and lifted the vehicle until he heard the child yell, "It's off of me." To put it in perspective, the world record for the deadlift, the exercise most resembling lifting a car off the ground, is currently 1,015 lbs., roughly one-third of what Tom lifted. Tom isn't a highly trained powerlifter with genetically superior size and strength. He's a regular guy. How did he do it? How could you do it?

The body uses two types of skills for physical activity. Fine Motor Skills, which are used for intricate tasks such as buttoning a shirt or putting a key in the car ignition, and gross motor skills which handle larger tasks like running and jumping. In periods of stress, pressure, or fear, the body's ability to use fine motor skills decreases, but the gross motor skills increase. Therefore, you often see people shaking without the ability to do small tasks when they are frightened and fearful.

Penn State kinesiologist Vladimir Zatsiorsky performed a study on weightlifters and learned that humans under normal circumstances only use about 65% of their strength. In periods of stress, the fear-response of the brain releases chemicals, analgesics, which numb the pain and allow the person under duress to perform at a higher capacity as a result of the stimulus that normally tells the brain "this hurts, stop," not firing.

In those same times of duress, the brain releases Norepinephrine, a form of mental adrenaline, that also helps the person enhance their focus in each situation. Sports psychologists often use techniques associated with the form of focus as it relates to anxiety and fear for athletes struggling with slumps and performance.

The point is, your body and your mind are capable of more than what you currently operate at. You may think to yourself, I don't want to have to lift a car to save a child, become an Olympic lifter, or fear for my life to improve performance, so how do I do it?

The simple answer and first step toward becoming an opportunity-creating monster is Love. Loving something deeper than yourself. Love, like fear, releases chemical adrenaline into your brain. In addition to the same Norepinephrine that is released during times of fear, the brain releases other chemicals such as Dopamine, which improves mood, motivation and reduces pain, as well as oxytocin which boasts a range of benefits ranging from quicker healing to muscle regeneration.

Simply put, by loving someone or something, you unlock strength inside yourself that your body and mind naturally limit in your day-to-day life.

EMBRACE INSTABILITY

We've all seen mild-mannered Clark Kent step into a phone booth and emerge in his famous blue-and-red uniform with the cape and the "S" on his chest as Superman, ready to save the day. Maybe we can't fly, but that doesn't stop us from being super! Have you ever been so focused on a task that others around you thought you were a machine? Athletes get in the zone; performers find their rhythm; analysts and businesspeople lock-in. Unlike the average person, the greats in any industry or genre can step outside their everyday selves and step *into* the super-version of themselves.

But why step outside of ourselves? Each of us has fears, limiting beliefs (as we discussed in earlier chapters), and perceived ceilings. But have you ever analyzed a problem that a friend was having and noticed that you had the answers for them, even though when you had the exact same problem — whether it be a relationship issue, financial dilemma, or another kind of problem — you couldn't fix it yourself? The reason is you were too close to the situation. It's hard to see all the facts when we look at it from a first-person point of view, but when we step outside ourselves, we lose the fears and limits because we become so laser-focused that we no longer see them. Therefore, they no longer exist. Like our bodies being able to rise above the self-regulating limits we place on ourselves to reach our peak state, so does intense focus allow us to push the boundaries of our mental capacity.

In their book Stealing Fire, Steven Kotler and Jamie Wheal discuss how to get into an optimal state of consciousness that allows you to focus and block out distractions and self-doubt. The focal point of the book is ecstasis, based on the Greek word ἔκστασις, meaning to stand outside one's self or a removal to elsewhere."

One of the main takeaways the authors discuss is that to train for stability in all situations, which is what we often desire, we must start with instability.

What we can derive from this concept as it relates to creating opportunity, is that in order to be our best peak-self in the day-to-day, we must be able to conjure up the "monster" version of ourselves. Because of the negative perception of the term "monster or beast," we fear being called one of these names because we don't want to appear unstable. However, growth and opportunity come stem from instability.

We discussed in the last chapter that the way to overcome fear is to repeatedly put yourself in the same situation or to step outside your comfort zone. By chasing the "unstable" state, you will push yourself to focus more. The only way ice-skaters get better and are able to execute more daring maneuvers is by embracing their instability on the ice and trying the leaps and spins until the instability becomes the norm. Weightlifters fight the resistance of weights until they don't feel the resistance anymore. When you're driving in a new part of town or in a new city, do you turn the radio down and focus on every streetlight and sign? By stepping outside the comfort of your normal commute, you will focus more on what's around you.

Embrace your peak mental state by focusing. Don't just tell yourself to focus, but step outside of your norms, a place outside of your day-to-day operations, a place that will require maximum focus. When you do so, you unlock the brain's natural ability to tune out distractions, gossip, "what others are saying," and any other intangible that isn't growth minded, and help you to unleash the Beast inside of you.

Root your growth and opportunistic mindset in the love of something deeper than yourself like the All-Blacks preparing for a match or the ancient Maori warriors preparing for war. Embrace the uncertainties and the instability of stepping outside of yourself, and you'll emerge a Superm¬¬¬an like Clark Kent out of the booth.

Become a monster, and opportunity will emerge.

CHAPTER 18
THE EXTRA DEGREE

Suppose I gave you two options: Option one is I give you $1M; option two is I give you one penny, and I'll double the amount every day for 30 days. If I told you that you had five seconds to decide, which would you choose? I recently surveyed 100 random people, and 94, without hesitation, said that they'd take the million dollars. Four out of the remaining six said that they had heard the riddle before.

In society, we often place extreme significance on "the now." In sports, we look at an athlete's height, weight, and other physical attributes. In business, we look at the strength of the company as it is right now. In the classroom, we judge students based on their current performance. I'm not saying these aren't important metrics. What I am suggesting, is that we place too much emphasis on the "now" point in time as a predictor of future performance.

But what about consistency? How much emphasis do we give to those that work hard daily as it pertains to long term success? If we focus on the "now" variables, we often miss it, but sustainable success is a direct factor of consistent improvement.

What I'm saying is this – if you want to create opportunity, your daily work, not some random act of chance or luck, is what gets you there. Simple mathematics proves this to be true. In the example I provided at the beginning of this chapter, I believe we can all agree it would be great luck to receive $1M randomly. That's why 94% of people selected that option. But, let's do the math on option two, the "consistently improving" option. If you start with one penny and double it every day after for 30 days, here's how it would look.

Day 1: $.01

Day 2: $.02

Day 3: $.04

Day 4: $.08

Day 5: $.16

Day 6: $.32

Day 7: $.64

Day 8: $1.28

Day 9: $2.56

Day 10: $5.12

Day 11: $10.24

Day 12: $20.48

Day 13: $40.96

Day 14: $81.92

Day 15: $163.84

Day 16: $327.68

Day 17: $655.36

Day 18: $1,310.72

Day 19: $2,621.44

Day 20: $5,242.88

Day 21: $10,485.76

Day 22: $20,971.52

Day 23: $41,943.04

Day 24: $83,886.08

Day 25: $167,772.16

Day 26: $335,544.32

Day 27: $671,088.64

Day 28: $1,342,177.28

Day 29: $2,684,354.56

Day 30: $5,368,709.12

If you selected the second option, you'd be more than five times richer than the person that selected the easy million dollars. But why then, do so many seemingly pick the first option in life? You may be thinking, no one has given me those two options, but they do. How many times have you taken a job or stayed in a career that you know you're more advanced than, just because it was less stress or work than working toward a better one? Have you ever stayed in a relationship longer than you should or allowed a friend to remain in your life well after you've realized they no longer served as an asset or positive force in your life? Perhaps you say, "oh, that's just how he/she is" as an excuse for their bad behavior because it's easier to stay around people who know you than to go through the whole process of meeting new friends and growing relationships.

Our lives are filled with areas where we "take the million." There are two trains of thought as to why we do this. 1) It's easy, convenient, and guaranteed, and 2) we don't believe in ourselves enough to follow through in the long term. If you look at the table above, you'll realize it takes 28 days of consistent improvement to reach what you could have received with no work on day one. Because life is unpredictable and perhaps are progress doesn't always double-daily, we think it's a no-brainer to take what's easy because it is guaranteed.

But for those select few of us – the few who are willing to bet on ourselves and value maximizing our long-term potential vs. taking the easy route; those of us who make it to Day 29 and Day 30 – that's where the opportunity resides. Simply put, the opportunities we are trying to create for ourselves lie a step, a day, or a mile past the finish line of convenience. Opportunity comes from understanding that success is far from linear – and that's the beauty of it! If we learn to wait it out and continue to improve, then opportunity will reap many rewards. You look at the money example above, on Day 29, you may say, "Wow, in one day, I improved on that million dollars by over 2 1/2 times. On Day 30, I quintupled my earnings over the original million." But is that true? Is it only one or two days that brought you all the extra worth? On paper, that's what you see because that's what most people see. But what truly led to those money-making opportunities was a culmination of all the momentum from the previous 28 days.

It starts with what we do on day one — compounded by the next day, and every day afterward — that will get us the results we truly desire.

WHO'S THAT GUY?

Tom Brady is a household name. Tom, the quarterback for the New England Patriots, is a six-time Super Bowl champion, a multiple MVP and All-Pro selection, and he boasts the record for most wins by a quarterback in NFL history. Many regard Tom Brady as the greatest of all time. What's even more impressive is that 42-year-old Brady is entering his 20th season as of the writing of this book. To put this astonishing feat into perspective, according to the NFL Players Association — the body responsible for looking out for the players' best interest — the average career of an NFL player is 3.3 years. Brady's career has been longer than six times the average.

So, what is It about Tom Brady that is so special? You might think, he must be fast and strong or have an amazing arm, or a slew of other all-star caliber physical traits to be able to withstand the grueling NFL season and continue to put up impressive statistics. If you didn't know anything about him and just saw his stats now, you'd assume that he was always naturally gifted and was a statistically elite player that just continued his legendary journey. But that would be incorrect. In fact, Brady almost didn't even get drafted.

Every spring, the teams from the National Football League gather for the annual Draft. The Draft is set up so that each of the 32 NFL teams gets 8 picks, divided out amongst seven rounds over a couple of days. There are 256 total picks and of the eight picks per team, the odds of a draft pick making the actual team, which has a limit of 53 total players, dwindles the further back the player is selected. Statistically, slightly less than half of all players in round 6 or 7 make the NFL roster.

When selecting players to draft for their team, NFL owners and scouts typically evaluate two types of criteria. First, they look at the athlete's college career. Those with an illustrious career filled with record-breaking statistics and highlights are often shoe-ins for first-round picks. First-round picks usually get the big endorsements, guaranteed contract money, and signing bonuses.

The second criterion often used by scouts is the NFL Combine. The NFL Combine occurs weeks before the Draft and tests the speed, agility, strength, and skill of the NFL hopefuls in a myriad of drills. Arguably the most important drill at the NFL Combine is the 40-yard dash. The NFL is largely based on speed, so a great 40 time can improve your draft status; a poor time can hurt your status. Many careers have been made or lost based on this drill.

To have such a great career, Tom Brady must have at least had a decent 40 time, right? Wrong. Tom Brady ran an abysmal 5.28 second 40. To put it in perspective, the average speed of Offensive lineman, the protectors of the quarterback that often weigh in excess of 300 lbs., is 5.30. Therefore, in a 40-yard race, Brady would barely beat most NFL lineman, and several of those linemen would beat Brady. Since the 2000 NFL Draft, only three quarterbacks since then have ran a slower time than Tom.

The NFL scouting report consensus for Tom Brady labeled him, "*Poor build, skinny, lacks great physical stature and strength, lacks mobility and ability to avoid the rush, lacks a really strong arm, can't drive the ball downfield and does not throw a tight spiral.*" Not exactly elite-quarterback numbers. Well, if his Combine wasn't good, then he must have had a stellar career in college, right? Wrong! Unlike most NFL quarterbacks, who led their team on the field for the majority of their career, Tom Brady never got the chance to be the sole leader of his team. His college coach at the University of Michigan ran an unusual system that had Tom Brady switching out every quarter with the younger Drew Henson. Essentially, Tom Brady was a part-time quarterback.

But the New England Patriots took a chance. In the 6th round, the 199th pick of the 2000 draft, they selected Tom Brady. The odds said he wouldn't make the team. After all, The New England Patriots had a superstar Quarterback already in Drew Bledsoe and didn't need a replacement. At the very best, Tom Brady could be a good backup quarterback to help in practice, most thought.

But veteran assistant Dick Rehbein, the new quarterbacks' coach for the New England Patriots, saw something no one else saw. He didn't look at the "what you see now, easy million-dollar" traits, for if so, Tom Brady wouldn't have been the guy. He saw a guy who was willing to work from Day 1 to double his worth daily to be the greatest. Rehbein didn't look at the fact that his stats weren't the best, and his physical attributes lacked, he looked deeper and saw Brady knew how to win.

In scouting Brady, he noticed that everyone at Michigan loved his leadership qualities, something you can't see on a statistics sheet. Though he had limited opportunities, several times, Tom Brady entered the game from behind and led his team to victory. He learned that Brady was the first to practice and the last to leave, always willing to put in the extra work to be the best. On top of that, Brady was fiercely competitive. He once gave a pep-talk to his team to make sure they didn't lose a charity exhibition game to local firefighters. Brady was willing to do anything it took to win and demonstrated that daily.

The day of the Draft, it showed. After being selected 6th, which as I mentioned before, gives athletes about a 50% chance of actually making the team, and a far lower chance of playing any meaningful snaps, Brady walked directly over to the Patriots Owner, Robert Kraft, and said, "I'm the best decision this organization ever made."

In the second game of his second year, after backing Up All-Pro Drew Bledsoe, Brady got a chance to prove that. In that game, Drew Bledsoe was injured on a play when being tackled by New York Jet's linebacker Mo Lewis. When the star quarterback goes down, most teams are almost guaranteed failure for the remainder of the season. Tom Brady buckled his chin strap, ran into the game, and told his teammates in the huddle, "Bledsoe isn't getting his $*&#^(@ job back."

Eighteen seasons later, he has not relinquished his job as the starting quarterback and all-time greatest quarterback in the NFL. It isn't physical traits or athletic intangibles that make Brady great. It's his relentless daily work ethic that has cast him to the forefront of greatness.

He's known for his inhumanly strict diet, going to bed at 8:30 pm daily, working out at 5:30 am before all his teammates get to the practice facility, and using brain games to keep his mind sharp each night.

The key to championship opportunity is to focus on systematic, day-to-day habits, knowing that those habits and actions — when compounded over a career — will warrant results far greater than you could get by simply taking what's easy and convenient. What are you doing to work toward compounded results?

THE ONE DEGREE

Water is the most unique substance on Earth. Its uniqueness comes from the fact that it's the only substance on Earth that can transform into all three states. In its normal form, it's a liquid. If it gets to 32 degrees Fahrenheit (0 degrees Celsius), it freezes and becomes ice. At 212 degrees Fahrenheit (100 degrees Celsius), it converts into steam.

I observe this phenomenon every morning as I wait for the water to boil to brew my French Press Coffee. Over the course of those few moments, the water goes from still to slight bubbles forming near the surface until final large bubbles break the surface and stream flow out of the kettle. Fascinating that at 211 degrees, it's simply hot water but that one extra degree added, and the water turns into steam and evaporates into the air.

But is it that one degree, the 212th degree, that makes all the difference? That degree is the degree that scientists studied to determine at what point water boiled. That's the degree, where if we watch the water on a thermometer, we see change. That's the degree that gets the credit. Similarly, we always see when the latest tech mogul goes public with his company and becomes an instant billionaire. We watch highlights of our favorite sports hero as they hit the shot or make the play that sends them into the record books. We celebrate the moment of birth as a new baby comes into the world.

But is it that day the company goes IPO, the last play that set the record, that moment when new parents see their baby, or that final degree to reach a boiling point that is the most important? Sure, those are monumental moments, but what are they without all the days and plays that proceeded them? Is the baby born without spending numerous months growing inside the mother? Does an athlete reach the point record without all the other baskets, goals, or touchdowns before that? Does water reach a boiling point without the other 211 degrees of heat before it?

Opportunity understands that the culmination of attempts, work, and days before opportunity is realized as equally as important as the day that opportunity arrives. The more you put into each day, the stronger the results of future opportunities will become. In the example, we shared at the beginning of the chapter, what would happen if you started with more than one penny, aka what if you put more into that day? What if you put in more than double each day? You would get exponential results. Creating a platform for opportunity is simply giving the most to each day KNOWING that ultimately, you'll create a multiplier effect and far surpass the "Good opportunities" and "decent results" and instead reach the potential and maximized results you deserve.

All degrees in heating water are equal. All the "doubling" efforts of a penny each day are equal. All of Tom Brady's consistent habits and daily hard work are equal. The result of equal, day in and day out hard work, multiplied over time, are results and opportunities far beyond the "now" results you gain from inconsistency, luck, or chance.

The best way to guarantee that opportunity and the outcome of your dreams will arrive tomorrow is to maximize today — *every day.*

CHAPTER 19
BECOME THE GLUE

We all remember going to elementary school with our brand-new backpacks filled with supplies, including pencils, scissors, construction paper, crayons (the big box with the sharpener if you were a rich kid), and Elmer's glue. We all loved the glue. I think I speak for everyone when I say that we couldn't wait for the days when we got to do crafts, just so we could use the glue. Don't you remember putting it on everything? We'd let it dry on our fingers to peel it off. We'd put it on the construction paper to glue things together; yet it never seemed strong enough to hold our elementary inventions. We loved glue.

In an earlier chapter, we discussed the importance of asking "how does it work" when we examined the inner workings of a Rolex watch as it pertains to our skillset. I asked myself the same question about glue, "how does it work?" The answer holds one of the final clues to creating opportunity.

Nowadays there are more glues than you can imagine. Gorilla glue, Wood glue, Super glue, glue Sticks, Adhesive glue, and every other type of glue you can imagine or not. Each has their traits and nuances, but at the essence of how glue works is fascinating, and will no doubt help you create opportunity in your life.

Before we get into glue, it's imperative that you have a basic understanding of how magnets work. All magnets are charged, typically with one side positive and the other side negative. If the substance the magnet is trying to connect to has the opposite polarity, aka if the positive side of the magnet faces the negative side of another magnet or other object such as a refrigerator, the magnet sticks together. Opposites do indeed attract. If, however, you try and connect two sides of a magnet that are the same (take two magnets off your refrigerator now and try and force the dark ends of the magnet to connect) and you'll find the magnets repel each other. No matter how hard you press the magnets together, they simply won't connect because they both share the same charge and have no way of connecting. Simply put, too much of the same thing removes any chance of a real connection.

From a bird's eye view, glue and other adhesives are filled with molecules that possess both positive AND negative charges concurrently. When glue is applied to a surface, it finds the small pores in the surface of the other object, and the negative and positive molecules go to work filling the crevices and connecting with other molecules. Since the glue is made of positive and negative charges, it can connect with the other surface no matter what. The less smooth the material the glue is being applied to is, the easier it is for the glue to stick because there are more pores in the material.

Think about your face at the end of the day when your pores are open and filled with gunk just waiting to be washed off. If you've ever had a facial, you'll realize very quickly how much build up is stored in these pores. Glue penetrates the pores of the material it's being applied to. It connects with opposing charges creating the bond that makes the glue work. The reason glue has a hard time connecting to smooth surfaces such as glass, is smooth surfaces don't have many pores, so the glue has no opposite charged molecules to connect to.

Now imagine what would happen you became the glue in your situation. Magnets see "positive vs. negative" and act accordingly. Likewise, modern society sees "good vs. bad", "black vs. white", "skinny vs. fat", "rich vs. poor", "democrat vs. republican", and countless other opposites. But glue doesn't view it that way. Glue understands that it possesses a little bit of everything and to be successful at its job, the opposite is needed.

D0 you view the world that way? Too often, we want to surround ourselves with people who are like us, who share our interests, and think the way we do. That's an easy way to stay comfortable. It's also a surefire way to remain mediocre and live below your potential. We must behave in a manner that not only looks for differences but appreciates the "opposites" in life because the "opposites" are how we bond. The opposites are needed to bring out our best qualities. Opposites help us connect; opposites help us grow stronger.

Becoming the glue will place you at the center of your career, your social circle, your community, and your family. The Great Wall of China — and some of the most prolific skyscrapers in the world — were built with innumerable bricks. But without the mortar holding them together, the walls would fall.

Change your mindset. Appreciate the differences around you. Those differences are necessary for growth. The world isn't black and white, but where it's black, exude white. Where it's white, exude black. Possess the opposite skill, opposite talent, the opposite viewpoint of the situation or job you're in. I'm not suggesting you walk into a good situation and bring the bad, but I am challenging you to bring a new perspective, a new idea, or new methodology to your career, family, or standard way of living.

You don't have to be the brightest, strongest, smartest, or best to create opportunity. You simply need to be the connection between all the pieces around you. A simple Lego, comprised of a raised (positive) side and sunken (negative) side, can create monuments when stacked accordingly. By becoming the glue or the Lego, you don't look at life in terms of opposites being bad, but rather you seek to fill a void when you can, and you seek to have voids filled when possible.

To create opportunity, you don't have to stand out. Remember, what was the key to LEGO's success that we discussed in Chapter 4? It wasn't built on some extreme technology; it doesn't require advanced knowledge of how it works to use. LEGO is simple and interconnected. Therein lies its power. Therein lies opportunity.

You must become the piece that binds everyone together. Become the DNA of your family, your office, and your community, and opportunity will become endless. People need air to breathe, water to survive, and glue to hold us all together. Become the glue.

CHAPTER 20
IT'S CLOSER THAN YOU THINK

I grew up idolizing NFL greats of the time, such as Warren Moon, Jerry Rice, and Herschel Walker. The neighborhood kids and I always gathered in the front yard for a game of tackle football with our plastic helmets and pads, emulating our heroes. It was never fair. I always stacked the teams. Maybe it was because I wanted to ensure victory or maybe my friends and I were more athletic than the other kids. In either scenario, we never lost. We won so much that the other kids stopped coming over to play against us.

We needed new competition. My nine-year-old brain thought long and hard about who we could lure into the Front Yard Football League, FYFL, to take a loss at the hands of my elite squad and me. One day, I had the answer. I'll get my six-year-old sister, Kierstan, to play. As an already emerging elite athlete in soccer, my young sister took the challenge. We outfitted her with a plastic Hutch Helmet and plastic shoulder pads and told her the game rules. My team would kick the ball off, and she would have two options. First, she could catch the ball and try and run it back to the driveway for a touchdown.

Second, if she didn't feel like she'd be able to run it for a touchdown, then when she caught the kickoff, she could take a knee.

What I failed to explain to my sister was that you can only take a knee when you catch it, not any time after. Forget that we didn't give her any teammates or blockers; forget that we were stronger, more experienced, and outnumbered her. We kicked the ball off; she caught it and began to run. She took off down the side of the front yard nearest the street.

I had the angle on her. I was going to deliver a hit for the ages, one that the pre-YouTube era kids would talk about in folklore forever. As I gathered myself and sprung at my sister, ready to knock her into oblivion, something happened. Recognizing that she wasn't going to make it to the endzone — and sensing impending doom as her older brother flew through the air with every ounce of his being — she took a knee. As a result, I flew over her, my arms grasping only air, and I landed with a thud on the street.

My teammates stood there, motionless, appalled at what had just transpired. On paper, I should have been victorious. I was better equipped, more knowledgeable, and physically superior. If you were to bet, it's safe to say the bets would have been on me to be victorious. However, on that fateful day, my sister taught me the cornerstone lesson on opportunity that shaped the entirety of this book.

Opportunity is not about being bigger, faster, stronger, or giving maximum effort; sometimes, it's just about identifying where it is. She couldn't outrun me, she wasn't strong enough to shake off a tackle if we collided, but she realized she didn't have to. Opportunity favors those that prepare for it, that identify it, that take advantage of it when it presents itself. Are you prepared? Do you know what it looks like? Do you focus on striking at the opportune time, or do you waste time thinking about all the tools and resources you don't have?

We look for opportunity as though it were Bigfoot or the Loch Ness monster — a mythic being or creature somewhere out there on the horizon. We hear about it, talk about it, and some even say they see it, but we seldom believe that we'll ever capture it. What my sister taught me is this: Not only is opportunity real, but it's also closer than you think.

SELL PIXELS AND SHOVELS

In the 1840s, gold was discovered in California, and a mass influx of would-be fortune seekers stormed an area near San Francisco in search of the gold. Miners from all over the United States stampeded to the area as newspapers across the country reported GOLD! The hunt for gold was so intense that local San Francisco businesses had to close their doors because their employees left their jobs to hunt for the heralded gold.

Everyone was mining for gold. Everyone that is, except for Sam Brannan, a storekeeper with the only shop between San Francisco and California Goldfields. Sam bought all the picks, shovels, and pans he could for as little as 20 cents apiece and sold them to the limitless fortune seekers for $15 apiece. As a result of not pursuing gold but rather selling to those who are seeking it, Sam Brannan became the first millionaire of the California Gold Rush.

Opportunity is closer than you think. Look at the path and trajectory you currently feel is necessary to reach your goal and ask yourself this. "Where along the path could I set up shop and capitalize on others in the same pursuit?" By helping others get to the same destination you're seeking, you'll find opportunity a lot quicker than most.

When you ask yourself the hard questions, take the limits off the preconceived notions of your potential and ability, you start to move toward opportunity. When you shift your mindset to understand you are built on a solid foundation with limitless potential and possess a unique toolset to succeed, your mind begins to awaken to the idea of opportunity. When you double down on those skills, sharpen those opportunity finders, learn how to strike, when to strike, and where, you're 90% of the way there.

Taking your knowledge and ever-growing skillset, you choose between finding an opportunity or creating it for yourself. In either situation, you rest easy and can build opportunity because you've now learned that opportunity isn't a coincidental or circumstantial ideal reserved for a select few. Opportunity is abundant and nearby. It may be as simple as taking a knee when the rest of the world is rushing by.

At the end of the day, it's important to remember this.

You are and always will be the opportunity.

ABOUT THE AUTHOR

Baylor Barbee, M.S.Ed, is a best-selling author, award-winning speaker, triathlete, and host of the popular podcast, "Shark Theory". Known for his engaging style and ability to shift audiences' perspective to find opportunities in their lives, Baylor's message has been trusted by several Fortune 500 companies, universities, and large-scale nonprofit organizations in the world.

As founder of his Mindset Development company, Shark Theory LLC, Baylor has spoken and led training and development seminars for many respectable organizations such as Chase, Xerox, the Texas Department of Criminal Justice, Boys & Girls Club of America, and Paul Mitchell. He has also consulted many startups and businesses founded by professional athletes in the NBA and NFL.

A versatile speaker and author with Amazon best-selling books in genres including depression, faith, relationships, and motivation, Baylor inspires diverse audiences to remove mental barriers, build sustainable confidence and administer strategies for growth.

His podcast, Shark Theory, takes everyday situations and gives listeners action steps toward finding freedom in their business, personal, and fitness lives.

Baylor's philosophy can be summed up with one of his most popular quotes: "When my body gets tired, my mind says, 'This is where winners are made.' When my mind gets tired, my heart says, 'This is where champions are made.'"

As a former scholarship football player for Baylor University and current endurance athlete, Baylor draws upon experiences in both competition and life to give audiences insight into peak-performance. In constant pursuit of victory, Baylor strives to liberate audiences from the mental setbacks, fears, and other traps that prevent personal and professional success.

His message has taken him from corporate boardrooms and maximum security prisons to podiums in front of elite level athletic teams as organizations look to him to develop winning mindsets in their leaders and teams.

A strong believer in the importance of education, Baylor holds both an undergraduate and a master's degree from Baylor University. He was named by the Dallas Convention and Visitors' Bureau as one of the Top 12 Most Influential African-Americans in Dallas, Texas, and he was ranked by the DataBird Research Journal as one of the Top 100 Business Keynote Speakers.

A former Division 1 scholarship athlete, Baylor played football for Baylor University, where he earned a BBA in Marketing & Entrepreneurship, and a master's degree in Education.

Learn more about Baylor at www.BaylorBarbee.com or visit his company site at www.SharkTheory.com

ACKNOWLEDGEMENTS

Over the two years I've spent writing this book, this is perhaps the hardest section to write. How do I begin to say thank you when words don't adequately express the level of gratitude that I have for all those who have helped me on this journey? So many people have had a profound impact on the themes, ideas, and contents of this book and on the consciousness that helped manifest these pages.

Those who know me also know that I'm often seemingly sporadic and unconventional in my approach to life. In that same manner, these acknowledgments come in no particular order but with my highest regards and gratitude.

To Andre Emmett: Thank you for the lessons, great times, and love that you showed me. I'll continue pushing your legacy, putting good vibes into the world, and showing everyone that dreams really exist.

To my dad: Thank you for showing me what it means to be a man and to work hard to provide for others. Your daily "Habit Lifters" have shaped my mindset over these last few years and given me a positive perspective to begin each morning while working on this book.

To my mom: Thank you for supporting me and

believing in me — even during the times when it didn't make sense to do so. Thank you for teaching me what it means to compete and win.

To my sister Kierstan: Thank you for helping me see the beauty in chasing the sunrise and for showing me what it means to live life with a heart of gold.

To my brother Britton: You're a prime example of what happens when you commit to a plan and work hard. I love seeing the life and family that you've built. I cherish our daily convos more than you know.

To Brandi: Thank you for being a wonderful wife to my brother, a wonderful sister to me, and a wonderful mother to the best nephews and niece I could ask for — Bailey, Carter, and Beckett. The greatest gift I have been given in life is the opportunity to have you all as my immediate family.

To Connie Marquez and Raymond Basye: The prayers that you send me mean more than I could ever express and have undoubtedly had an immense role in my success.

To Kevin Bush: The scriptures, wisdom, and positive energy you share with me truly encourage me.

To Michael "Captain Sharky" Marquez: Thanks for helping me stay focused on catching the big fish in life. #ItsAMonsta

To Jasmin Brand, thank you for the years of putting up with me, staying patient as I grew, giving me sound advice, listening to all my crazy dreams, and helping me formulate strategies to make them come true.

To Kristal Sharp: You represent the epitome of a great soul. Thank you for all that you've done, for the love that you've shown me, and for listening to me practice my TED Talk 85 million times. Because of your caring heart and consistency, I have no doubt that you'll change the world. You've definitely helped change mine.

To Rich Mendoza: Seeing the empire you're building inspires me daily. I appreciate you for always being someone whom I can count on for anything, and I look forward to showing the world what a couple of kids from small towns in West Texas are capable of accomplishing.

To Dary Stone: Thank you for your friendship and for showing me the importance of fighting for what's right and standing up for what you believe in. Our Saturday mornings as a basketball family are the most cherished part of my week.

To Le'Shai Maston and Robin Jones: Thank you for your words of wisdom, humility, and kindness, and for being all-around great men. Y'all are brothers to me.

To Julian Placino and Marques Roberts: Seeing your careers as speakers flourish brings me more joy than you can imagine.

To Chris Hudson: Thanks for the consistent reminder to start local and finish global.

Without a focus on health and wellness, no one would be able to enjoy the benefits of opportunity. I'm thankful to those who continue to help me on my fitness journey by providing both consistency and friendship:

- To Destenee Dowd: I never would have known an hour on a stair-stepper was even possible without you and our weekly #TortureTuesdays.

- To Tricia Dennis: Thank you for your friendship and for helping me understand the importance of nutrition. I love seeing you flourish in your career, but I miss those morning Starbucks and conversations.

- To Mercedes Owens: Your positive energy is infectious; thank you for making fitness fun.

- To Bree'Anna Lucero (aka Breezy): Your consistency in preparing and winning Europa NPC, your daily commitment to your health, and your constant reminder that we're "blessed to see another one" has helped me more than you realize.

- To Elizabeth Miller: I'm amazed by seeing you grow from someone who was just thinking about getting into running into someone who has crushed a marathon and finally into someone who is now teaching others how to do it. Your journey inspires me.

- To Stephanie Hanson: Thank you for the years of friendship, for believing in me, for pushing me, and for creating plans to help me succeed in these crazy Ironman Triathlons.

To Ashley Fulks: Of all the great things that I have learned from you, your constant reminder that it's okay to "feel feelings" ranks at the top. Thank you for embodying what it means to be compassionate and empathetic toward others and for showing me that life doesn't always have to be about success, competition, and winning. Sometimes, the greatest victory is being present with loved ones and enjoying each other's company.

To Kennith Smith: What you built through your hard work is remarkable and serves as a daily reminder of the opportunities that come with consistent hard work.

To J.J. Salomon and Sherman Jameson: Thanks for serving as examples of what it means to make big moves. I've learned a lot.

To Danny Andino: Thank you for being a living example of what happens when you combine faith with obedience and hard work. Proud of you, brother.

To Landon Ledford: Thanks for instilling the "People Helping People" philosophy in my life.

To Mat Macko: Thank you for opening doors for me. I am forever grateful for our brainstorming/therapy dinners.

To Nichole Geigley: Thank you for all that you've done. I always look forward to my Phoenix trips because of you and John.

To Mark Carroll and Joao "Somalia" Pedro: Literally flipping my world upside-down in my one-and-only Brazilian Jiu-Jitsu class had a profound impact on my perspective in life and served as a cornerstone lesson of this book. Thank you.

To Dalton Ruer: Who would have ever thought that a Wintality Mindset would have connected us? Thank you for your unwavering support.

To Ashish Dev: From the first time I met you, and you told me about the "Mile 19" in your life, and the adversities you defeated to come from Nepal and succeed in America, I was impressed. Seeing you organize your own TEDx Event and granting me the honor of speaking at it meant the world to me. You're destined for greatness.

To Asja Jordan: I love seeing you create opportunities for yourself with Potential 2 Kinetic. You're an inspiration.

To Christine Schaible, Jasmin Eales, and Melisa Andino: Thank you for loving and believing in me — even during the times when I doubted myself. I wouldn't be who I am today without you.

To Nicole Been: Thank you for your love, support, and commitment to your cause. I learned so much from you about what can happen when you passionately fight for what you believe in.

To Emily LeGendre: Thank you for the laughs, the crazy stories, and your energy.

To Jenn Karsner: Thank you for never quitting on yourself. Your drive inspires me daily.

New Opportunity would mean nothing if it wasn't rooted in consistency. I'm beyond grateful for those who not only had my back before anyone knew who I was, but who continue to show me the same level of support, loyalty, and friendship today. Thank you for riding with me through the ups and downs, the highs and lows, and the triumphs and trials.

- To K.B Stevenson: Thanks for being a true ride-or-die brother. Even in my more egotistical days, you had my back and continue to do so today. I can never repay you for that loyalty.

- To Shoni Power: Thank you for your belief in me. So many times, you believed in me more than I believed in myself, and that drove me to succeed. Your courage and strength in fighting this second round of breast cancer — all while continuing to uplift and inspire others — is a consistent reminder of what a superhero you are. It's an honor to have Wonder Woman as a best friend.

- To Brittany Prier: I'll never forget those long, late-night drives just dreaming about the great things we wanted in life. Thank you for your loyalty and for never turning your back on me, whether I was right or wrong. Your presence in my life brings me joy.

- To Brie McFarland: There's no one I'd rather race with than you. Thank you for being a true friend — even since back in the BU days.

- To Alina Adatia: I could write a book on my thankfulness for how great you've been to me over the years. Thank you for giving me a greater world perspective, your undying support, and so many amazing memories.

- To Amy Arredondo: I've always adored your smile and your kindness. Although the restaurants we used to frequent to talk about life in no longer exist, I'm thankful that our friendship continues to grow

To Rory, the world's best Yorkie: I love you. Thank you for showing me the importance of looking at each day as a fresh new start.

To the librarians who have helped me with my research for this book; the thousands who have listened to my talks, keynotes, and lectures as I crafted and tested the material for this book; and the countless people who have shared my words, viewed my posts, or listened to my podcasts: I'm forever grateful.

To Abbey Decker: Thank you for the edits, suggestions, and work you put into cleaning up the countless grammatical mistakes this manuscript had and turning it into a work of art that I am truly proud of.

And last but not least, thank YOU. Your time is valuable, and it means the world to me that you devoted some of it to reading this book. It is my sincerest hope that you will find and create abundant opportunity for yourself and those you love.

My deepest gratitude to you all,

Baylor Barbee

REFERENCES

1. Number of jobs, labor market experience, and earnings growth: Results from a national longitudinal survey [PDF File]. Retrieved from https://www.bls.gov/news.release/pdf/nlsoy.pdf

2. Bates, Lucy A. & Poole, Joyce H. & Byrne, Richard W. Elephant Cognition. Current Biology Vol 18 No 13. Retrieved From https://www.cell.com/current-biology/pdf/S0960-9822(08)00503-4.pdf

3. Ritchie, James. Fact or Fiction?: Elephants Never Forget. Retrieved from https://www.scientificamerican.com/article/elephants-never-forget/

4. Elephant Emotions. Retrieved from http://www.pbs.org/wnet/nature/unforgettable-elephants-elephant-emotions/5886/

5. Gaffey, Connor. Elephants never forget and barely sleep either. Retrieved from https://www.newsweek.com/elephants-never-forget-and-barely-sleep-562710

6. Schelling, Ameena. This Is How Baby Elephants Are Trained For The Circus. Retrieved from https://www.thedodo.com/baby-circus-elephant-training-1695763541.html

7. Frei, Georges. Elephant Training and Dressage in the zoo and circus. Retrieved from https://en.upali.ch/training/

8. Reuben, Stephen Carr. What Baby Elephants Can Teach Us About Human Freedom. Retrieved from https://www.huffpost.com/entry/what-baby-elephants-can-teach-us-about-human-freedom_b_2452099

9. Mandel, D. R. (1995). Chaos theory, sensitive dependence, and the logistic equation. American Psychologist, 50(2), 106–107. https://doi.org/10.1037/0003-066X.50.2.106

10. What is Chaos Theory? Retrieved from https://fractalfoundation.org/resources/what-is-chaos-theory/

11. Werndl, Charlotte (2009). "What are the New Implications of Chaos for Unpredictability?". The British Journal for the Philosophy of Science. 60 (1): 195–220. arXiv:1310.1576. doi:10.1093/bjps/axn053.

12. Tim, Palmer. "The Butterfly Effect - What Does It Really Signify?". Oxford U. Dept. of Mathematics Youtube Channel.

13. Kounang, Nadia. "What is the science behind fear?" Retrieved from https://www.cnn.com/2015/10/29/health/science-of-fear/index.html

14. Thorp, Tris. "Deconditioning: How to Create Pattern Interrupts and Learn New Behaviors." Retrieved from https://chopra.com/articles/deconditioning-how-to-create-pattern-interrupts-and-learn-new-behaviors

15. Mcleod, Saul. "Cognitive Dissonance." Retrieved from https://www.simplypsychology.org/cognitive-dissonance.html

16. Eysenck, Michael (2012). Attention and Arousal : Cognition and Performance. Berlin, Heidelberg: Springer Berlin Heidelberg. ISBN 978-3-642-68390-9. OCLC 858929786.

17. Schacter, Daniel L.; Addis, Donna Rose; Buckner, Randy L. (2007). "Remembering the past to imagine the future: the prospective brain". Nature Reviews Neuroscience. Springer Nature. 8 (9): 657–661. doi:10.1038/nrn2213. ISSN 1471-003X. PMID 17700624.

18. Goff LM, Roediger HL (1998). "Imagination inflation for action events: Repeated imaginings lead to illusory recollections". Memory and Cognition. 26: 20–33. doi:10.3758/bf03211367.

19. Garouphalias, Petros (1979). Pyrrhus: King of Epirus. London, UK: Stacey International. ISBN 0-905743-13-X.

20. Richard, Carl J. (2003). Twelve Greeks and Romans who Changed the World. Oxford, UK: Rowman and Littlefield Publishers, Incorporated. ISBN 0-7425-2791-3.

21. Tomm, Sara. How to Develop Muscle. Retrieved from https://www.sportsrec.com/552572-how-to-build-tear-down-muscle.html

22. Marano, Hara Estroff. Why We Love Bad News. Retrieved from https://www.psychologytoday.com/us/articles/200305/why-we-love-bad-news

23. Brain Neurons & Synapses. Retrieved from https://human-memory.net/brain-neurons-synapses/

24. Chudler EH. "Brain Facts and Figures". Neuroscience for Kids. Retrieved from http://faculty.washington.edu/chudler/facts.html

25. How Many Neurons Are in the Brain? Retrieved from https://www.brainfacts.org/in-the-lab/meet-the-researcher/2018/how-many-neurons-are-in-the-brain-120418

26. Giles, Lionnel. Sun Tzu On The Art Of War. Abingdon, Oxon: Routledge, 2013.

27. N, Kate. The Magic of 21 Days. Retrieved from https://www.empathia.com/the-magic-of-21-days/

28. Maltz, Maxwell. 1976. Psycho-cybernetics: a new way to get more living out of life. N. Hollywood, Calif: Wilshire Book.

29. How Long Does it Actually Take to Form a New Habit? (Backed by Science). Retrieved from https://jamesclear.com/new-habit

30. Grohol, John M. Need to Form a New Habit? Give Yourself At Least 66 Days. Retrieved from https://psychcentral.com/blog/need-to-form-a-new-habit-66-days/

31. Reuben, Gretcehn. Stop Expecting to Change Your Habit in 21 Days. Retrieved from https://www.psychologytoday.com/us/blog/the-happiness-project/200910/stop-expecting-change-your-habit-in-21-days

32. Morin, Amy. How Cognitive Biases Influence How You Think and Act. Retrieved from https://www.verywellmind.com/what-is-a-cognitive-bias-2794963

33. Dobrow, Julia R. & Gidney, Calvin L. The Annals of the American Academy of Political and Social Science Vol. 557, Children and Television (May, 1998), pp. 105-119

34. Blakemore, Erin. The Disastrous Backstory Behind the Invention of LEGO Bricks. Retrieved from https://www.history.com/news/the-disastrous-backstory-behind-the-invention-of-lego-bricks

35. Brick by Brick: The Lego Story. Wisconsin Public Radio. 25 December 2013.

36. LEGO history. Retrieved from https://www.lego.com/en-us/lego-history

37. How does sonar work? Retrieved from https://www.exploratorium.edu/theworld/sonar/sonar.html

38. "Radar of the Deep - SONAR", November 1945, Popular Science.

39. Taylor, David A. Smithsonian Magazine. The History of the Doughnut (March 1998)

40. The Maine Ship Captain Who Invented the Modern Donut. Retrieved from http://www.newenglandhistoricalsociety.com/maine-ship-captain-invented-modern-donut/

41. Pulmonary edema. Retrieved from https://www.mayoclinic.org/diseases-conditions/pulmonary-edema/symptoms-causes/syc-20377009

42. O'Brien, Barbara. What Are the Four Noble Truths of Buddhism? Retrieved from https://www.learnreligions.com/the-four-noble-truths-450095

43. Damien Keown (2013). Buddhism: A Very Short Introduction. Oxford University Press. pp. 48–62 (Chapter 4: The Four Noble Truths).

44. Carol Anderson (2004). Robert E Buswell Jr (ed.). Encyclopedia of Buddhism. MacMillan Reference, Thomson Gale. pp. 295–297.

45. How Aspens Grow. Retrieved from https://www.fs.fed.us/wildflowers/beauty/aspen/grow.shtml

46. Georgiou, Aristos. Pando Aspen CLone: World's largest single organism is dying on mankind's watch. Retrieved from https://www.newsweek.com/pando-aspen-clone-worlds-largest-single-organism-dying-mankinds-watch-1176411

47. Lindell, John. Facts on Aspen Trees. Retrieved from https://sciencing.com/aspen-trees-6120998.html

48. Kevin Fedarko, Mark Thompson, Edward Barnes, Ann Blackman, Greg Burke, Dan Cray, Douglas Waller (June 19, 1995). "Rescuing Scott O'Grady: All For One". Time Magazine.

49. Francis X. Clines (June 9, 1995). "Conflict in the Balkans: The Rescue; Downed U.S. Pilot Rescued in Bosnia in Daring Raid". New York Times.

50. Bagley, Rebecca O. The Key to Growth: Transformational Change. Retrieved from https://www.forbes.com/sites/rebeccabagley/2013/01/02/the-key-to-growth-transformational-change/#18d6fe896b8c

51. S-Shaped Growth Curve. Retrieved from https://www.encyclopedia.com/earth-and-environment/ecology-and-environmentalism/environmental-studies/s-shaped-growth-curve

52. Berger, Eric. Inside the eight desperate weeks that saved SpaceX from ruin. Retrieved from https://arstechnica.com/science/2018/09/inside-the-eight-desperate-weeks-that-saved-spacex-from-ruin/

53. Kumparak, Greg; Burns, Matt; Escher, Anna (January 4, 2013). "A Brief history of Tesla". Tech Crunch. San Francisco, California: Verizon Media.

54. Tobak, Steve (April 11, 2014). "Trust Your Own Focus Group of One". Entrepreneur.com. Retrieved April 21, 2014. Elon Musk, founder of PayPal, Tesla and SpaceX.

55. Vance, Ashlee (2015). Elon Musk: Tesla, SpaceX, and the Quest for a Fantastic Future. New York City: Ecco Press.

56. Griffiths, Jack. The Daring Ones: Italy's Arditi were the knife-fighting shock troops of World War I. Retrieved from https://www.historyanswers.co.uk/history-of-war/the-daring-ones-italys-ardriti-were-the-knife-fighting-shock-troops-of-world-war-i/

57. Ricci, Paolo. Mountain fighting was hell for Italy's elite WWI shock troops. Retrieved from https://www.wearethemighty.com/arditi-world-war-i?rebelltitem=1#rebelltitem1

58. Pirocchi, Angelo. Italian Arditi: Elite Assault Troops 1917–20. Osprey Publishing.

59. The Science behind the Punch. Retrieved from https://boxingscience.co.uk/science-behind-punch/

60. Johnny N. How To Take Punches Better. Retrieved from https://expertboxing.com/how-to-take-punches-better

61. Vera, Marita. The Science of a Boxing Knockout. Retrieved from https://www.popularmechanics.com/adventure/sports/a6372/boxing-knockout-sports-science/

62. Newton's Laws of Motion. Retrieved from https://www.grc.nasa.gov/www/k-12/airplane/newton.html

63. Newton's Three Laws of Motion. Retrieved from https://ccrma.stanford.edu/~jos/pasp/Newton_s_Three_Laws_Motion.html

64. XE Currency Converter. Retrieved from https://www.xe.com/currencyconverter/convert/?Amount=1&From=USD&To=PEN

65. Hubble Space Telescope. Retrieved from https://hubblesite.org/

66. About the Hubble Space Telescope. Retrieved from https://www.nasa.gov/mission_pages/hubble/story/index.html

67. Why Are Mountain Goats Such Effective Climbers? Retrieved from https://www.forbes.com/sites/quora/2017/05/26/why-are-mountain-goats-such-effective-climbers/#76103f6e237a

68. Tennenhouse, Erica. How Mountain Goats Ascend Nearly Vertical Cliffs. Retrieved from http://thescienceexplorer.com/nature/how-mountain-goats-ascend-nearly-vertical-cliffs

69. Harrington, Rebecca. Mountain goats have incredible cliff-climbing skills — here's how they do it. Retrieved

from https://www.businessinsider.com/mountain-goats-climbing-cliffs-how-do-they-do-it-2015-10

70. Woodford, Chris. Night Vision. Retrieved from https://www.explainthatstuff.com/hownightvisionworks.html

71. How Does Night Vision Work. Retrieved from https://www.atncorp.com/hownightvisionworks

72. Ault, Alicia. Ask Smithsonian: How Does Night Vision Work? Retrieved from https://www.smithsonianmag.com/smithsonian-institution/ask-smithsonian-how-does-night-vision-work-180956656/

73. Fischer, Jake. How Red Panda Became the NBA's Favorite Halftime Performer. Retrieved from https://www.si.com/nba/2019/08/28/red-panda-rong-niu-nba-halftime-china-76ers-warriors

74. Mita, Molly. "A woman whose journey has been almost as incredible as the act that's earned her millions of fans." Retrieved from https://www.espnfrontrow.com/2019/05/a-woman-whose-journey-has-been-almost-as-incredible-as-the-act-thats-earned-her-millions-of-fans/

75. Red Panda. Retrieved from https://agt.fandom.com/wiki/Red_Panda

76. PERPETUAL MOVEMENTS. Retrieved from https://www.rolex.com/about-rolex-watches/movements.html

77. Altieri, Paul. A Closer Look at What Makes the Iconic Rolex Oyster Perpetual Movement Tick. Retrieved from https://www.bobswatches.com/rolex-blog/resources/a-closer-look-at-what-makes-the-iconic-oyster-perpetual-movement-tick.html

78. Cartwright, Mark. Samurai. https://www.ancient.eu/Samurai/

79. Katana 'Soul Of The Samurai' – Most Famous Japanese Sword With Long Tradition. Retrieved from http://www.ancientpages.com/2018/04/12/katana-soul-of-the-samurai-most-famous-japanese-sword-with-long-tradition/

80. Samurai and Bushido. Retrieved from https://www.history.com/topics/japan/samurai-and-bushido

81. Samurai. Retrieved from https://www.pbs.org/empires/japan/enteredo_8.html

82. Department of Asian Art. "Samurai." In Heilbrunn Timeline of Art History. New York: The Metropolitan Museum of Art, 2000–. http://www.metmuseum.org/toah/hd/samu/hd_samu.htm (October 2002)

83. Kanzan Sato (1983). The Japanese Sword: A Comprehensive Guide (Japanese arts Library). Japan: Kodansha International. p. 220.

84. Secrets of the Samurai Sword. Retrieved from https://www.pbs.org/wgbh/nova/samurai/swor-nf.html

85. Herkewitz, William. The Science of the One-Inch Punch. Retrieved from https://www.popularmechanics.com/science/health/a3093/the-science-of-bruce-lees-one-inch-punch-16814527/

86. Jeet Kune Do. Retrieved from https://brucelee.com/jeet-kune-do

87. Lee, Bruce (September 1971), "Liberate Yourself From Classical Karate", Black Belt Magazine, Rainbow Publications, Inc., vol. 9 no. 9, p. 24

88. Lee, Bruce (2008). Bruce Lee's Fighting Method. Valencia: Black Belt.

89. Lee, Linda (1975), The Tao of Jeet Kune Do, Ohara Publications Inc.

90. Murphy Jr., Bill. GM Has a 2-Word Dress Code, and It's Actually Brilliant. Retrieved from https://www.inc.com/bill-murphy-jr/this-giant-company-has-a-2-word-dress-code-its-actually-kind-of-brilliant.html

91. Feloni, Richard. GM CEO Mary Barra explains how shrinking the dress code to 2 words reflects her mission for the company. Retrieved from https://www.businessinsider.com/gm-ceo-mary-barra-on-changing-gms-dress-code-2015-3

92. Anderson, Joel. Mike Leach to teach seminar titled 'Insurgent Warfare and Football Strategies' at Washington State. Retrieved from https://www.espn.com/college-football/story/_/id/26057093/mike-leach-teach-seminar-titled-insurgent-warfare-football-strategies-washington-state

93. The History of Diamonds. Retrieved from https://bebusinessed.com/history/history-of-diamonds/

94. Scarratt, Kenneth and Shor, Russell. The Cullinan Diamond Centennial: A history of Gemological Analysis of Cullinans I and II. Retrieved from https://www.gia.edu/doc/SU06A2.pdf

95. Imagine discovering the world's largest diamond, the Cullinan. Retrieved from https://www.capetowndiamondmuseum.org/blog/2017/01/worlds-largest-diamond-the-cullinan/

96. Cullinan Diamond. Retrieved from http://www.cullinan-diamond.com/

97. Achilles. Retrieved from https://www.history.com/topics/ancient-history/achilles

98. Achilles: The Trojan War. Retrieved from https://

www.greekmythology.com/Myths/Heroes/Achilles/ achilles.html

99. Homer. Iliad. London : New York :Dent; Dutton, 1955.

100. Sigmund Freud, On Metapsychology (PFL 11) p. 276-7

101. Laplanche, Jean; Pontalis, Jean-Bertrand (1988) [1973]. "Pleasure Principle (pp. 322-5)". The Language of Psycho-analysis (reprint, revised ed.). London: Karnac Books.

102. Pleasure Principle. Retrieved from https://www. goodtherapy.org/blog/psychpedia/pleasure-principle

103. Why does the ocean have waves? Retrieved from https://oceanservice.noaa.gov/facts/wavesinocean. html

104. Wave Formation. Retrieved from https://www.eoas. ubc.ca/courses/atsc113/sailing/met_concepts/08-met-waves/8a-wave-formation/index.html

105. Waves. Retrieved from https://courses.lumenlearning. com/boundless-physics/chapter/waves/

106. What causes ocean waves? Retrieved from https:// oceanexplorer.noaa.gov/facts/waves.html

107. Leblanc, Chris. Going to the Ground: Lessons from Law Enforcement. Journal of Non-lethal Combatives (January 2007). Retrieved from https://ejmas.com/ jnc/2007jnc/jncart_Leblanc_0701.ht

108. Cognitive Dissonance. Retrieved from https://www. psychologytoday.com/us/basics/cognitive-dissonance

109. Festinger, L. (1962). "Cognitive dissonance". Scientific American. 207 (4): 93–107. Bibcode:1962SciAm.207d..93F. doi:10.1038/ scientificamerican1062-93. PMID 13892642.

110. Festinger, L. (1957). A Theory of Cognitive Dissonance. California: Stanford University Press.

111. "Interpersonal Communication and Relations | Cognitive Dissonance theory". Universiteit Twente.

112. Festinger, Leon. A Theory of Cognitive Dissonance. Stanford University Press.

113. Groves, Lee. Mike Tyson-Trevor Berbick: 30 Years later. Retrieved from https://www.ringtv.com/474524-mike-tyson-trevor-berbick-30-years-later/

114. Sandford, Daniel. Mike Tyson destroyed Trevor Berbick to become the youngest world heavyweight boxing champion. Retrieved from https://talksport.com/sport/boxing/632806/mike-tyson-trevor-berbick-boxing-champion-1986/

115. Status quo.TheIdioms.com - Online Idioms Dictionary

116. Dr. C. Michael Botterweck. "Glossary for Sociology 100". academics.triton.edu

117. Craft, A. (2001). Neuro-linguistic programming and learning theory. The Curriculum Journal, 12(1), 125-136. doi: 10.1080/09585170010017781

118. Neuro-Linguistic Programming (NLP). Retrieved from https://www.goodtherapy.org/learn-about-therapy/types/neuro-linguistic-programming

119. Pattern Interrupt. Retrieved from https://www.nlpworld.co.uk/nlp-glossary/p/pattern-interrupt/

120. Pattern Interrupt: Redirect Your Thoughts In An Instant. Retrieved from https://dailynlp.com/pattern-interrupt/

121. Bandler, Richard & Grinder, John. Neuro-Linguistic Programming™ and the Transformation of Meaning. Real People Press.

122. Broeniman, Clifford (1996). "Demodocus, Odysseus, and the Trojan War in "Odyssey" 8". The Classical World. 90 (1): 3–13. JSTOR 4351895.

123. Homer, Odyssey, 4. 274-289.

124. Wood, Michael (1985). In Search of the Trojan War. London: BBC books. pp. 80, 251

125. Eric H. Cline (2013). The Trojan War: A Very Short Introduction.

126. The Real Trojan Horse. S14 Ep3. Retrieved from https://www.pbs.org/wnet/secrets/real-trojan-horse-full-episode/2316/

127. Bigelow, Joe (1933). "King Kong review". Variety.

128. Hall, Mordaunt (March 3, 1933). "King Kong". New York Times.

129. Young, Rob. Eight Little-Known Facts About King Kong. Retrieved from http://www.cinelinx.com/movie-news/movie-stuff/eight-little-known-facts-about-king-kong/

130. Barr, Jason (2016). The Kaiju Film: A Critical Study of Cinema's Biggest Monsters. McFarland.

131. Edwards, Gareth (2014). Godzilla. Warner Bros. Pictures.

132. Shelley, Mary Wollstonecraft, 1797-1851. Frankenstein, Or, The Modern Prometheus : the 1818 Text. Oxford ; New York :Oxford University Press, 1998.

133. Kerr, James. Legacy. Hachette Book Group.

134. Whelan, David. Talking Rugby and the Haka with Maori Cultural Expert Inia Maxwell. Retrieved from https://www.vice.com/en_us/article/jmaaep/talking-rugby-and-the-haka-with-maori-cultural-expert-inia-maxwell-au

135. HAKA - MĀORI WAR DANCES. Retrieved from https://www.newzealand.com/us/feature/haka/

136. Pōmare, Mīria (12 February 2014). "Ngāti Toarangatira – Chant composed by Te Rauparaha". Te Ara – the Encyclopedia of New Zealand. Ministry for Culture & Heritage.

137. "A Famous Haka", March 1959, Rev. Tipi Kaa, Te Ao Hou The New World

138. "The new All Blacks jersey – a tribute to history". All Blacks. 30 July 2011.

139. Disney's Beauty and the Beast. Racine, Wis.: Western Pub. Co., 1991.

140. Wise, Jeff. Yes, You Really Can Lift a Car Off a Trapped Child. Retrieved from https://www.psychologytoday.com/us/blog/extreme-fear/201011/yes-you-really-can-lift-car-trapped-child

141. Hansman, Heather. Love Can Make You Stronger. Retrieved from https://psmag.com/social-justice/oxytocin-muscle-regeneration-orgasm-love-can-make-stronger-89231

142. Wu, Katherine. Love, Actually: The science behind lust, attraction, and companionship. Retrieved from http://sitn.hms.harvard.edu/flash/2017/love-actually-science-behind-lust-attraction-companionship/

143. Keegan, Sheila M. The Psychology of Fear in Organizations: How to Transform Anxiety into Well-being, Productivity and Innovation.

144. Zatsiorsky, Valdimir M. & Kraemer, William J. Science and Practice of Strengh Training. (2006)

145. Kotler, Steven & Wheal, Jamie. Stealing Fire. Harper Collins. (2017)

146. Lewis, Charlton T. & Short, Charles (1879) A Latin Dictionary, Oxford: Clarendon Press

147. Gaines, Cork. "How the Patriots pulled off the biggest steal in NFL history". Business Insider. Business Insider.

148. "Lessons from Tom Brady's Recruiting in College". NCSA Athletic Recruiting Blog. Retrieved from https://www.ncsasports.org/blog/2015/11/17/high-school-football-players-learn-tom-bradys-recruiting-process/

149. Jenkins, Lee (January 31, 2008). "Self-made man". Sports Illustrated.

150. Davis, Scott. 41 examples of Tom Brady's extraordinary competitiveness. Retrieved from https://www.businessinsider.com/tom-bradys-insane-competitiveness-examples-2017-8

151. O'Connor, Ian. Meet Tom Brady's first believer. Retrieved from https://www.espn.com/nfl/playoffs/2014/story/_/id/12175963/dick-rehbein-championed-tom-brady-new-england-patriots

152. Babb, Kent. This coach convinced Bill Belichick to draft Tom Brady. Retrieved from https://www.washingtonpost.com/sports/this-coach-convinced-bill-belichick-to-draft-tom-brady-now-his-daughters-keep-his-memory-alive/2018/02/02/b610ce94-0820-11e8-8777-2a059f168dd2_story.html

153. Craig, Mark. Former Vikings assistant was early Tom Brady believer. Retrieved from http://www.startribune.com/former-vikings-assistant-was-early-tom-brady-believer/470815663/

154. Boiling Point of Water and Altitude. Retrieved from https://www.engineeringtoolbox.com/boiling-points-water-altitude-d_1344.html

155. Helmenstine, Anne Marie. What Is the Boiling Point of Water? Retrieved from https://www.thoughtco.com/what-is-the-boiling-point-of-water-607865

156. Boiling Point. Retrieved from https://www.britannica.com/science/boiling-point

157. What makes adhesives sticky? Retrieved from https://home.howstuffworks.com/adhesives-sticky.htm

158. Woodford, Chris. Adhesives (glue). Retrieved from https://www.explainthatstuff.com/adhesives.html

159. Layton, Julia. How Adhesive Tape Works. Retrieved from https://science.howstuffworks.com/innovation/everyday-innovations/adhesive-tape1.htm

160. Samuel Brannan: Gold Rush Entrepreneur. Retrieved from https://www.pbs.org/wgbh/americanexperience/features/goldrush-samuel-brannan/

161. Sam Brannan, California's First Millionaire. Retrieved from http://wordpress.napahistory.org/wordpress/sam-brannan-californias-first-millionaire/?doing_wp_cron=1576097364.8267600536346435546875

162. Weiser, Kathy. "CALIFORNIA LEGENDS Old Sacramento - Walking on History". LEGENDS OF AMERICA.

OTHER WORKS BY THE AUTHOR

BOOKS

WINTALITY:
Unlock Your Success DNA

IDEA OF EXCELLENCE:
The Pursuit of Purpose, Passion, & Performance

SEE MY HEART, NOT MY PAST

PODCAST

If you're looking for inspiration, perspective,
or mindset development, check out Baylor's podcast,
"Shark Theory," on all podcast platforms

for more information,
visit www.BaylorBarbee.com

CPSIA information can be obtained
at www.ICGtesting.com
Printed in the USA
LVHW110037180220
647168LV00023B/15

9 780578 622934